PUBLISHING
Pomona, CA 91799

To the four parents
who gave us a spiritual heritage

TOGETHER AT HOME

First Focus on the Family Publishing printing 1988

Library of Congress Cataloging-in-Publication Data

Merrill, Dean.
Together at home.

1. Christian education of children. 2. Children—Religious life. I. Merrill, Grace. II. Title.
BV1475.2.M47 1988 249 87-83353
ISBN 0-8499-3897X

Published by Focus on the Family Publishing, Pomona, CA 91799

Distributed by Word Books, Waco, Texas.
First printed by Thomas Nelson Publishers, 1985.

Printed in the United States of America

88 89 90 91 92 93 / 10 9 8 7 6 5 4 3 2 1

CONTENTS

Part One
Getting Started

Forming Young Christians: The Best Six Years

This book is for moms and dads of grade-school children—approximate ages six to twelve. It is a resource for raising Christian kids.

We wrote it because we don't think that's impossible.

Neither do we think you have to be an expert to pull it off. Too many parents these days have been spooked into thinking they're incompetent, especially when it comes to expressing their faith. *Don't look to ME to tell them about God. That's the minister's/ religion teacher's job. They know how.* And they do (usually).

But so can we—ordinary parents. We can reclaim our franchise. In fact, if we don't, it may not matter too much what the religious experts try because our kids may not be listening.

Yes, we know parents are awfully busy these days, and in a great many homes the mom holds an outside job as well as the dad... while in other homes there's only a mom (or only a dad). Yet, whatever the arrangement, those in charge desperately want their children to grow up not only with clean ears and teeth but also clean minds and hearts, fit for a responsible adulthood.

The two of us happen to believe the grade school years are prime time for instilling Christian values. The trouble is, that's about the time many Christian parents *quit.* Once they get past the preschool days of "read me a story," parents seem to be unsure of what to do next. The bedtime Bible storybook is now dog-eared, and the child can read for himself anyway.

But the best times are yet to come. Springtime is now turning into summer, when the child's spiritual life grows fastest and easiest in the warm sun... building strength, rising tall, spreading its leaves, gaining stamina for harsher seasons ahead.

Are we talking about daily devotions at the dinner table, "family altar," and so forth? No. That is an honorable tradition, and we salute it. We also know some families where it flourishes today.

A younger version has come alongside in recent years, however: the weekly family night. Households that never seemed to be able to manage a daily observance have found new vigor in this format.

How does it work? That's what the first chapter of this book is all about. Then comes a small encyclopedia of ideas for use on such a night.

But actually, there are other uses as well. Families can use these ideas on a more ad hoc schedule. For example, this book can go along on vacation for special times in the car, around campfires, or in cabins at night.

Teachers, club leaders, and pastors (the "experts"!) may also sneak an idea here or there for use in the groups they lead.

On the cover, we promised you "A Proven Plan." What does *proven* mean? It means we didn't just sit down and think up a bunch of proposals that "ought to work."

Every idea in this book has been tried in at least one family—ours. We've gone back to our family night logbook, which we started in December 1977, and built this material straight from our records. That's why, in a number of cases, we tell you about our family, our experience, our kids, who said what, how things worked. Not to be talking about ourselves. . .but to let you know the context of these times together and what you might expect at your house.

There are actually sixty-one units in this book, but many units contain two or more ideas for individual family times. Use them freely. Adapt them. Change them around. Make them fit your personality, your sibling mix, your climate, your theology, your goals. Milk these ideas for whatever they're worth toward the raising of a new generation of young Christians.

Time Out for Nurture

During the late twentieth century there lived a sincere Christian couple with 2.4 lovely children. The husband and wife enjoyed the usual amenities of modern living, but unlike some of their neighbors, they were loyal adherents of a faith called Christianity.

"We want our kids to grow up to love God," they said, and they meant it. Toward that end, they made sure the household was up early on Sunday (the appointed day of worship) and that the children arrived at church in time for special classes. They gave their money in support of the church, and when the wife brought home children's books and records from the local Christian bookstore, the husband complained not at all about the cost.

The years went by, and in time, the children fulfilled their parents' wish, one even becoming a minister.

By now you have figured out that the above story is a fable—in more ways than one. The raising of a new generation of Christians is hardly so automatic. It is a complicated enterprise—more complicated than any of us dreamed back at the start of the first pregnancy—and there are few guarantees.

We certainly had few strategies in place when our firstborn arrived back in 1972. His twin sisters came (with only ten days' notice that there would be two, not one!) in early 1975; and in those early years, we were both so busy changing diapers and tugging with snowsuits that we thought only fleetingly about spiritual development. We read them bedtime books about Jesus, of course, and sprinkled the days with Christian music. But we hardly had the energy to consider an overall plan on top of everything else. There would be plenty of time later on.

We were bumped off dead center when Nathan trotted off to

kindergarten one fall and struck up a friendship with Derek, who lived on the other side of our block. Derek's family was Mormon. We found that out the day Grace made the mistake of calling Mrs. Van Orden and inviting Derek over to play the following Monday afternoon.

"No, Derek isn't free after school on Mondays," she kindly replied. "That's our Family Home Evening. All the children go to the ward meetinghouse for clubs in the late afternoon, and then we spend the evening together as a family. How about a different day?"

That made us decide it was high time for us to get up and moving. Although we didn't share their doctrine, we had to salute their system. It was time to start putting our actions where our convictions were.

We invited the Van Ordens over for dessert one night, mainly to quiz them about what they did on Mondays. They hardly fit our stereotype of Mormons. Here were modern, suburban parents (he a successful display designer in downtown Chicago) who talked excitedly about the mix of games, food, projects, and teaching they enjoyed with their children every seven days. After they left, we began to lay our own plans.

Advent was coming, and it gave us the launch we needed. Each week we gathered around the wreath, lit the candles, and talked and sang about Jesus' coming to earth. Nathan was five; Rhonda and Tricia were two and a half, and mesmerized by the flickering light. We mixed in some other activities and gave it all a name: "Home Together Night." When January came, we didn't want to stop.

As this book is released a decade later, our son is fifteen and our girls have just turned thirteen. Home Together Night has been part of their lives for as long as they can remember, because we believe:

- That modern families are split up most of the week, each person going his or her separate way, and that families need to be *together* at least a few quality hours each week to preserve unity.

- That a child's spiritual input ought not to come entirely from outsiders. Thank God for pastors, Sunday school teachers, club leaders, and all the rest—but their efforts are not enough. No matter how much they talk, the child still sits and mulls a silent question: *I wonder what my folks think of all this? Preachers and teachers are supposed to spout all this God stuff—that's their job. But does my dad buy this? My mom?* Parental silence may mean consent, but consent is not enough to make a difference in a kid's value system. We have to *say* some things.
- That kids are worth a block of uninterrupted, quality time each week. (No? If not, why not?)
- That Christian truth doesn't have to be boring. It can be alive, effective, and can blend with other forms of family sharing. It doesn't have to be closeted off in a holy zone of formality.
- That the family is the perfect size for effective teaching. The adult-child ratio is enough to make an educator drool. What Sunday school teacher wouldn't love this setting compared to twenty moving targets?
- That the generation gap can be bridged if we really care and are willing to reach out. Like most parents, we looked into the fresh faces of our preschoolers and hoped against hope that we could stay one another's friends through the storms of adolescence. The words of Derek's father keep echoing in our minds: "The prophets of our church have promised us that if we give our children this time each week as they're growing up, we won't lose them when they're teenagers. We will have built up a bank of trust to carry us through the later years."

In our house, we've dedicated Tuesdays as our special evening, from the time Dad arrives home from work until 8:30 or so. It has obviously meant adjusting our adult patterns—but could we honestly stand before God someday and claim we couldn't carve two or three hours out of 168 per week for concentrated parenting? Is that too much for children to expect? No.

Before going any further, let us stop and admit: *This is not the only way to raise Christian children. We are not saying we have found THE answer to fulfilling one's calling as a Christian father or mother.* We are saying, "Here is a way to match actions with precepts in the contemporary setting. If you're going to do *something* to inculcate your Christianity in your children (and we desperately hope you will), here's one format to check out."

The options from which we build each Home Together Night are varied. The only constants are the meal and the spiritual sharing/teaching; the others come and go. Here are some of the possible ingredients:

Food

The evening begins with a good meal—"good" by a kid's definition. Hamburgers instead of liver. Pizza instead of casserole. This is *not* the night to try to teach everyone the virtues of asparagus.

The location of the meal is sometimes varied, from outdoor picnics to the Ping-Pong table to the dining room for china and candlelight. *Just for kids?!* Why not? Who said finery was for outsiders only? Aren't kids special too? One way to let them know is to put on the Ritz for them occasionally.

On the other hand, one night we carted the food to somebody's bedroom, just to be crazy. A blanket in front of the fireplace can serve the same purpose. One night Grace stunned us all by withholding the silverware; it was fingers or nothing. Fortunately, the menu was fried chicken, french fries, finger Jell-O, relishes, and cupcakes.

The best meal, however, is a frustration to a child if the *conversation* swirls over his head. Therefore, we decided early that table talk would be exclusively kid talk on Tuesday evenings. No office politics. No heavy financial discussions. Instead, school talk, baseball talk, jokes, riddles, news about friends and bikes and dogs and dolls.

At one point, Grace filled a green Tupperware container with a hundred or more questions written on the backs of outdated business cards of mine: "The funniest person I ever met was. . ." "What's your favorite place on earth?" "Name something you especially enjoy at church." "What do you think parents should not do?" She gathered many of these from "The Ungame" and other resources, then thought up more of her own. Virtually every week, the green jar goes around the table along with the Jell-O and the crunchy carrot sticks, each person taking a card and starting a new round of answers (five rounds in all at our house, one for each family member).

Games

Breathes there a kid who doesn't enjoy playing a game with his parents? And breathes there a parent past fifty who doesn't regret taking so little time for games when the kids were young?

Games are parables of life. They teach us in visible ways about competing, concentrating, bearing down, not giving up, winning, losing—all vital lessons for the real world. Therefore, family members playing games together are hardly wasting time; they are enjoying one another and learning how to respond to life's realities.

The choice of games has varied from "Go Fish" to "Bible Challenge" to "Monopoly" to soccer to catch to "Frisbee," depending on the weather and the kids' preferences.

By now you have probably noticed that we mix the "secular" with the "sacred," the "fun" with the "religious," so kids don't know the difference. That is intentional. We *don't want* our kids putting God in a Sunday/church box. We want them bumping into God every time they turn around, in the midst of ordinary living. That way God will stay a normal, here-and-now part of their lives in adulthood.

Excursions

Too many families think only of $100 extravaganzas to an amusement park, which few can afford more than once a year. Meanwhile, they miss the fun of a trip to an ice-cream shop, a band concert in the park, a toboggan slide, a swimming pool, the public library, a hike around a lake. Nearly every area has places the average family hasn't gotten around to seeing yet, and most of them are free. We just have to take notice.

Spiritual Sharing/Teaching

Sometime during the course of the evening we take ten minutes or so—often in a circle on the floor and therefore called "Circle Time"— for Christian input. Again, the possibilities are endless, from stories, skits, and pantomimes to serious Bible study with older children.

It's important that these minutes not be led exclusively by one parent or the other. Kids need to see that the faith is real to both Dad and Mom.

The best times have been when we've capitalized on something happening in our children's lives. One example: In October 1981, when the Tylenol killer was on the loose, we talked one night about why our world had such people in it, and why others were trying to mimic the treachery. Aren't people trustworthy? We read Psalm 14, which explained how our world has been basically ruined, and realized we needn't be surprised. Then we went on to read Psalm 15 and reviewed the way God wants us to live, even in a twisted society. Finally came the hard question: Could we stop and pray for the killer? We didn't feel like it emotionally. . . but after a pause, we bowed our heads together.

The main purpose of this book is to provide you with more ideas than you'll ever use for this portion of such an evening or for anytime you choose to become a verbal Christian with your kids. In churches and couples' retreats around the country, as we have made Home Together Night presentations, this is the point at which parents have most wanted help—especially once their children advance past the read-me-a-story stage. Most caring parents can think up their own menu, games, and excursions or can get ideas from a wide range of resources, both Christian and general. Everything from the local newspaper to books such as *Things to Do on a Rainy Day* or *Sanity in the Summertime*, to name just a couple, serve this purpose. Meanwhile, the Achilles' heel of most Christian homes is *getting verbal* about Christian truth, opening up our deepest beliefs in ways kids can understand. Hence, this book.

Outreach

We've made cookies and then taken them to a neighbor with a broken arm, gone to sing in nursing homes, made cards for those in hospitals—anything to model ministry close up so kids can get the feel of reaching out to those in need.

Praying

It is important to keep prayer natural, conversational, and tailored to the length children will appreciate rather than dread. We've found lots of ways to do this. At times, a prayer log has kept us organized, helping us list our requests and rejoice when we can check them off.

Crafts and Projects

This has ranged from assembling photo montages to creating a homemade game. Often the craft can be merged with the teaching and/or the outreach as a reinforcement—a Bible story montage, for example.

Music

Every member's instrumental ability can be put to use without embarrassment. Singing fits well not only at home but also in the car en route to some other aspect of the evening.

Snacks

Provided the meal wasn't a feast, a batch of popcorn or homemade ice cream finishes the evening with warmth and good will. (For even heartier laughs, leave the lid off the popcorn popper and let the kernels fly all over a sheet on the floor.) The way to a kid's heart is still through his stomach.

In all of this, two cardinal rules have served us well:

1. *Whatever we do, we will do together*—the five of us. We are split up enough all week long. This is the one time we regroup. We will do only those things that all family members consider enjoyable.

   For instance, Dean and Grace might like to stroll through a shopping mall looking for furniture. The kids, however, would find this to be drudgery. At one point Nathan's favorite game was "Monopoly." But it was too complicated for the twins. Hence, both of the activities were out of bounds on Home Together Night.

2. *We will not tolerate distractions.* Our togetherness is more important than the evening news, the day's mail, even the telephone. Hence, the TV is off (unless there's a program all of us would enjoy), and the phone goes unanswered. Radical? All we usually miss are people trying to sell air conditioning or aluminum siding anyway. Our friends know to phone us later in the evening. Meanwhile, the look of pride on our children's faces as they realize we consider them more important than the ringing telephone is a beauty to behold.

   We recently heard of a family in Cleveland that worked together, kids and parents, to make a recorded message for their telephone answering machine: "Hello, this is the Patterson house, and we're having our special family time right now, so we can't take your call. But if you'll leave your name and number. . ." Not a bad idea!

> Even kitchen cleanup waits. These hours belong to the Lord and one another, exclusively.

As Wayne Rickerson, the best spokesman for this concept we know, writes, "Children, even teenagers, need and value family time. However, the children will not call the family together. It is our responsibility as parents to see that we have a balanced Christian family life—one that includes regular family time!"[1]

We cannot promise any family that once it starts such a family time, things will always run smoothly. There have been times when the weather messed us up, forcing us to Plan B. A couple of times we've had to stop the festivities and discipline a child very sternly, then continue. Once or twice, we have shut down the rest of the night because of misbehavior—to the shock and dismay of our children. The next week, they were angels!

Most often when Home Together Night has faltered, however, it's been because the two adults in the house failed to think things through in advance, and chaos moved into the vacuum.

A family night can't be done out of the hip pocket. Parents must believe in it strongly enough to sit down twenty-four hours ahead and say, "What should we do this week? What would they enjoy? What does the Lord want us to emphasize at this point?" This crucial planning goes faster, of course, if you keep a collection of resources, everything from books such as this one to a folder of clippings to spark your thinking and planning.

As time goes by, the children begin to chip in ideas of their own. While parental planning is foundational, one of the kids often comes along to say, "Can I read this story I wrote in school?" or "May I play my new flute piece?" or "I've got a math trick I bet you guys can't figure out" or "I made up a game." They are reveling in the fact that Home Together Night is a comfortable, warm place for them to express themselves, to "show and tell" to the family. Not only are verbal skills being developed, but the child's self-image is being fed. They are owning the family-night experience for themselves; it has become more than an adult idea.

However, a family night is not likely to succeed without a firm commitment from the major breadwinner. In our case, our children are firmly in the habit by now, eager for Tuesday night to come. Grace is a believer as well and more or less naturally builds her week's activities around Home Together Night. The fellow who has to fight off business obligations and other conflicts is Dean. If he doesn't take Home Together Night seriously, no one else will.

And when we're tempted to say we're awfully busy and maybe we'd better skip this week, Rickerson's words bring us up short: "Each family has its own set of 'impossible circumstances' that hinder it from having enough family time. However, an irrefutable fact of life is that we do the things we feel are most important. If the family is at the top of our list of priorities, we will be able to find family time."[2]

A United States senator, in the midst of hot debate over school prayer legislation, went to fulfill a speaking engagement at a church men's breakfast. He told his audience about what was happening on the Senate floor and then asked how many present were in favor of classroom prayer. A forest of hands went up.

"Let me ask one more question," he said. "How many of you here have prayed aloud with your children at home in the last week?" The response could be tallied on two hands.

We have no right to ask public school teachers—or private ones, for that matter, or clergy, or anyone else—to do what we ourselves neglect.

---

[1] Wayne Rickerson, *Getting Your Family Together* (Glendale, Calif.: Regal, 1977), 10-11.

[2] Rickerson, *Getting Your Family Together,* 14.

Part Two
Special
Times
Together

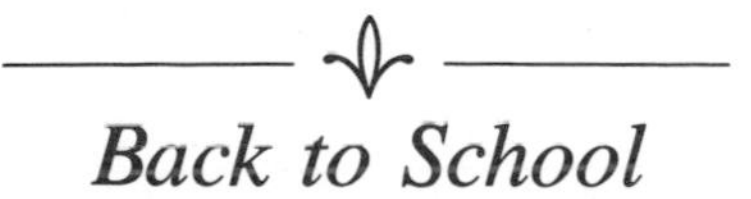

Back to School

The good news at the end of August is: They're going back to school (less direct responsibility for parents).

The bad news is: They'll be shoulder-to-shoulder with lots of non-Christians (unless they're enrolled in a Christian school).

The good news is: They're excited about growing up, taking the next step toward maturity.

The bad news is: They're a little scared, too.

This time of new beginnings is thus a window of special receptivity. Kids facing the unknowns of a new room, a new teacher, and a new mix of classmates are open to help from anyone, even parents.

So. . .

Start the family night with a back-to-school meal. Make place cards of black construction paper to represent a slate, with names written in chalk. If you have a small chalkboard, write the evening's menu on it and pass it around after the table prayer. Then use all the lunchboxes you can find for serving dishes. The kids will enjoy the uniqueness of filling their plates from lunchboxes. (Alternative: Have each lunchbox contain one person's meal in full.)

Center the table conversation around school, using such questions as:

- "What is a memory you have from kindergarten?"
- "What was your most embarrassing moment in school?"
- "When did you have your greatest feeling of accomplishment in school?"
- "What's one thing about *this* coming school year that you're glad about?"
- "What's one thing about this school year that concerns you?"

(Pay close attention to these last answers, and don't put them down as foolish worrying. You may want to change the rest of the evening's course as you uncover a deep apprehension that needs understanding and even prayer.)

Once the meal is finished, do something fun like a Handicap Spelling Bee. The year we did this, Grace, as the teacher, sat with a large dictionary. She gave the rest of us five cookies each and then began pronouncing words to be spelled. Only she chose them by level of ability: Rhonda and Tricia got words like *house* and *flag*, while Nathan got *radiology*—and Dean the editor had to contend with the likes of *phenylacetaldehyde!*

If you answered correctly, you got to eat one of your cookies. If you missed, you had to give a cookie to the person on your left. As you can well imagine, Dad went hungry, much to the delight of the other spellers. (Another way to stack the deck is to require the more advanced players to spell their words backwards.)

Finally, we talked about how kids and adults who know the Lord are sometimes called *people of the light*, since the Light of the World lives inside them. "As you go to school next Monday," we said, "you'll be one of the light-carriers. Some of the other kids and some of the teachers may be on the side of light, too, while many of them will be on the side of darkness.

"Which is stronger—light or darkness?" Obviously, as John 1:5 tells us, the light always overrides the darkness.

Then Dean continued, "Now I'm going to read a section from Ephesians 5 that tells people of the light how to act. Tricia, you stand by the wall switch, and whenever the verse talks about darkness or sin or anything negative, turn the light off. Whenever you hear anything about our side, turn the light back on."

We worked our way through verses 1-18, which portray the two life-styles in sharp contrast, back and forth. We closed with a family prayer that Jesus, the Light, would be visible in our lives the whole year.

This metaphor is one of the best, we think, to plant within Christian children. It carries the idea of being distinct from the non-Christian culture. It sets out a *wholesome* difference.

Another way to prepare children for the upcoming social pressures is to talk about three sea creatures with contrasting personalities. (Credit for this concept goes to a David C. Cook "Young Teen Action" elective course.)

Sharks are aggressive, pushy, and threatening.

Jellyfish are shy, non-assertive, unwilling to stand up for anything.

Dolphins are positive, assertive; they have no natural enemies in the sea. They always seem to be playing in the waves, but they've been known to sense a human being in trouble and rescue him from drowning by bobbing him back to the surface from underneath. However, the other fish don't try to mess with the dolphin. It can knock out even a shark with a sudden *thunk* of its head to the shark's belly.

This is a picture of any group of school kids. Some are loud, pushy, dangerous—like sharks.

Some, like jellyfish, are afraid to assert themselves, fearful of being noticed for any reason. And some are confident without being obnoxious. They take care of themselves; they do the right thing even if it's hard; they show courage.

A key Scripture for "dolphins" at school is 1 Corinthians 16:13—"Be on your guard; stand firm in the faith; be men [and women] of courage; be strong." Not a bad verse to memorize.

Do you have a picture book showing these three creatures? Use it to reinforce the descriptions.

If you have more time, you can illustrate each of the three styles using Old Testament characters: Saul (1 Sam. 18:5-12), Samson (Judg. 16:15-21), and Esther (Esther 4:15-16;7:1-6). Read about them from the Bible or a Bible storybook, and have your kids guess who's who.

Halloween Hype

We might as well admit at the beginning that October 31 is our least favorite holiday. Since we understand the Bible to teach that departed spirits go to be with either God or the Devil, we're not interested in trivializing these serious things. Halloween—who needs it?

But that's not the world of children. For these few years, they and their school friends think the night is marvelous.

Some Christian parents have chosen to ignore the whole hoopla, while at the opposite end of the spectrum, others revel in finding the scariest, spookiest costumes they can. We've tended toward the middle, allowing our children to do some modest candy-gathering from neighbors but drawing the line against anything even faintly occult.

As the kids have gotten older, we've made good use of Harold Myra's excellent book *Halloween—Is It for Real?* (Nelson), with its appealing story and lively Dwight Walles art. The author explains that although the holiday's roots are pagan, Christians came along and tried to change it from a time of fear to a time of joy. They called it "All-Hallow's Eve," and instead of focusing on ghosts, they thought about all the saints—true Christians—who loved God and were now in heaven.

But, of course, most of this has since been forgotten, and in the twentieth century we are back to paganism. The book's story winds up suggesting an all-saints party with a special time to remember specific Christians now with the Lord.

Not a bad idea.

Reading this book together led to some real soul-searching on the part of our girls, who were all set to be twin ghosts that year. "It doesn't mean anything—it's okay," said one. But her sister had doubts: "We don't want to be doing the same thing all those

Celts and Druids did, trying to look creepy so the evil spirits would think you were one of them.'' They finally decided that as Christians they were better off dressing up as a dog and a fat hobo.

We hadn't expected them to be this thorough—but we were delighted.

Before we bought the book, we spent Home Together Night one year reading a short story about Polycarp, the courageous bishop in the second century who was burned at the stake. He is best remembered for his final testimony: ''For eighty-six years I have been his slave, and he has done me no wrong; how can I blaspheme my king who has saved me?''

Another year we ate an orange meal (spaghetti, orange gelatin, and so forth), carved a big jack-o-lantern, and lit it. In the flickering candlelight we shared times we had been afraid (after a bike spill, when an animal threatened, while driving a car on ice). We thought of Bible people in similar predicaments: Abraham being asked to offer his son as a sacrifice, for example. Then, still staring at the pumpkin, we sang Psalm 27:1—''The Lord is my light and my salvation—whom shall I fear?''—with gusto.

Masks are another theme for Halloween discussion—the ways throughout the year we pretend to be what we're not. Are people fooled? Is God fooled? Then why go to the work of creating a ''mask,'' a false impression?

Then there was the year we joined with a number of other families at church for a fall party with lots of games, a pumpkin-decorating contest, and family skits. Our family selected David and Goliath. The twins were sheep, Mom was King Saul, Nathan was David, and his tall father was Goliath, complete with a cardboard armor decorated with a large red ''G'' a la Superman, a leftover fence picket for a sword, and a garbage can lid for a shield.

We know a family that preempts the entire holiday by taking off together for a special trip. They go to the city or to a hotel with an indoor pool; in this way they give their children so much attention and fun that a bagful of candy is pitifully poor competition.

We know of other homes where the parents and children work together preparing special treats to give out at the door—good candy plus a colorful, sensible gospel tract for children.

Each family has to make its own peace with Halloween. The important thing, we believe, is not just to float mindlessly with the culture. Make your choices, hold to your Christian values, clearly explain to your children why you feel the way you do, compensate for any take-aways with positive replacements—and don't get too pushy with other Christian parents who make different selections from yours!

Thanksgiving in a Gimme World

Why is Thanksgiving a second-class holiday to most North American children? The answer is obvious enough: no personal payoff, as on Christmas and birthdays. A big dinner is nice, but it hardly ranks with wrapped-up presents.

Thus, we face an uphill challenge to instill in our offspring some important but slightly abstract values: nonmaterialism, compassion for the needy, gratitude to others and to God. We would all like children to demonstrate these qualities. But they don't naturally grow like that. We have to coax the branch the opposite way. Here's how:

1. A nonmaterialistic attitude and life-style.

New Testament example: "Selling their possessions and goods, they [the believers] gave. . ." (Acts 2:45).

While the turkey is roasting and before the TV football game starts, sit down with your children and quietly page through a photo magazine that shows real life in an underdeveloped nation of the world. You can use either a general periodical such as *National Geographic* or *Life* (borrow it from your public library) or a Christian mission magazine such as *World Vision*. Read a story or two aloud; talk about what you see in the pictures.

Don't "hype" the misery; don't gush about "those *poor* people." Just let the facts speak for themselves. Then look up from the photos and pose the question, "What about us? In comparison to the world as a whole, are we poor? Medium? Rich?" See if you can nurture a world perspective regarding wealth.

(If you've been fortunate enough to travel overseas yourself, or have friends who have done so, you can make this little tour even more interesting by using your own pictures or those you've borrowed.)

One November we decided that to raise money for our church's "Project Manna" outreach at Christmastime, we would skip Monday night desserts. We also elected to cut out meat from one supper a week. Grace was commissioned to calculate the money saved by these measures and put it in a certain jar. When it was time to turn in the funds the week before Christmas, we'd saved a sizable amount.

This took such a small amount of *denial*—but denial is an oft-neglected virtue in our gimme world.

2. *True, heartfelt compassion toward others, especially the needy.*

New Testament example: " . . .They gave to anyone as he had need" (Acts 2:45).

Give each family member an unexpected dollar bill (or two dollars), a three-by-five card, and an envelope. The instructions:

"During the next week, buy or make something for someone outside our family, someone who's ill, or has some kind of need.

"Then write down on the card what you did, seal it inside the envelope, and bring it to Home Together Night next week. We'll talk about what was done."

You may have some objections to this idea, so let's discuss them:

Objection No. 1—*The child isn't spending his or her own money.* That's true. But the giving experience has to start somewhere. Children who see their parents hand out dollar bills to be given compassionately are more likely to start using their own funds than children for whom the whole idea stays theoretical.

Objection No. 2—*Children won't be able to follow through on this alone. They'll need ideas, a trip to the store, a postage stamp, and so forth.* That's also true. Nobody ever said sharing was a quick operation. (That's why even adults don't get around to it sometimes!) This will mean parental aid and assistance throughout the week. But again, what could be more important than showing a child how to read the needs of others and reach out to them?

When we did this at our house, one daughter made a school friend happy by buying a packet of stickers with the girl's name on them and slipping them into her backpack. Another child bought materials to make a decoration for the grandparents' apartment door. Grace made a pecan pie and left it on the doorstep of a neighbor; Dean spent his money on a coffee cake and dropped it at the teachers' lounge of Nathan's school on his way to work.

A different idea to extend compassion: Find a collegian who's not going home for the Thanksgiving holidays—perhaps an international student. Invite him or her to share your special meal with you. In this way you juxtapose the abundance of America with the poverty of the Third World all at the same table. Little eyes can hardly miss the point.

3. A general spirit of gratitude toward others.

New Testament example: "Every day they continued to meet together. . . with glad and sincere hearts" (Acts 2:46).

Sometimes we think the second most difficult English phrase to master (after "I'm sorry") is "Thank you." Even many adults can't seem to get the hang of it. They rarely breathe a word of appreciation when some kindness is shown them.

Children start out learning *Thank you* as a social pleasantry, but our larger goal is to make thankfulness a way of life for them, a ready response triggered anytime someone extends a gift or helping hand. Kids learn this, of course, by watching us in the off-moments—what happens when a casserole is brought to our home, when the family is invited out, when a neighbor helps fix the lawnmower. If we put our gratitude into words, and if we name our benefactors in prayer later on, we set the desired pattern.

In a more concrete way, family night is a good time to write appreciation letters to Sunday school teachers, youth club leaders, or some important individual in each family member's life. The letter doesn't have to be long, but what an effect it will have when it lands in the recipient's mailbox. It may even arrive at a crucial moment of discouragement in the Christian worker's ministry. (This is the kind of thing we all intend to do but don't get around to doing. Family night makes a time slot for getting around to it.)

One Tuesday night we planned a "Baby Sitter Appreciation Night." Mark and Nancy, a brother and sister, were favorite sitters for our children, so we created small homemade gifts for both of them and homemade invitations to join us a week later for pizza. The following week, instead of the usual "Hello—we'll be back at ten o'clock—goodbye," we spent a couple of hours face to face with these special teenagers. The family drove them to the Pizza Hut, then returned home to present our gifts and play a table game together.

They hardly knew what to make of such festivity; after all, baby-sitting is not a high-honors occupation. But we sincerely appreciated their service to our children, and we wanted to model that such service merits gratitude.

The same format will work with any esteemed person in your child's life.

4. Thankfulness to God himself.

New Testament example: "Every day they continued . . . praising God . . ." (Acts 2:46-47).

A long-standing tradition in our clan, started by Dean's mother, is to make place cards for the Thanksgiving meal—and to hide a Scripture reference on the underside. Each verse, when read before dessert, is an expression of thanks to God for his goodness. A Bible or two is passed around the table so each child and adult can add his or her Scripture to the litany.

(Hunting up the verses is a good exercise for the previous Home Together Night—or to keep kids out of the kitchen on Thanksgiving morning! All they need is a concordance and a quick lesson on how to find the "thanks" listing. Make sure they venture beyond Psalms for at least some of the selections.)

Even if non-Christian Uncle Howard is present at the holiday table, he can hardly object to reading a verse of Scripture, especially when seated next to an adoring niece or nephew who waits expectantly for the chain to continue.

Any meal during the last half of November may be a good time to quiz a child who's recently studied the Pilgrims in school. Why did they come to the New World? Why did they hold a Thanksgiving celebration? What happened? What was there to be thankful for? How did they find things to thank God for in such a harsh climate and with so little to live on? If your school tends to leave out this heritage, borrow a book from the library and read it aloud during one or more meals. Fill in the gaps in your child's education.

The classic, simple story from the life of Jesus that teaches thankfulness is, of course, the healing of the ten lepers (Luke 17:11-19). Quite young children have no trouble at all understanding the story line once it's read to them and figuring out how to playact the events. It can be done with as few as three characters (Jesus, the grateful Samaritan, and one too-busy-to-give-thanks member of the nine).

The night we did this, we used torn strips of an old sheet for bandages. Once the play was finished (with the obligatory rerun, of course), we sat in a circle and prayed thank-you sentences to God, going around the circle several times. Then we talked about how our daily praying should begin like this.

An alternative: Work together on an acrostic to list God's blessings according to the word *Thanksgiving—t*urkeys, *h*ealth, *a*llowances, and so forth. Write your acrostic on a large posterboard or chalkboard; then pray your way through it circle-fashion.

As we said in the beginning of this section, gratitude is more than just being polite. It is recognizing and honoring the Source of "every good and perfect gift" (James 1:17), thus helping children know their dependence upon a good and loving God.

Rx for the Christmas Carousel

Why is it we all seem to have sixty days' worth of Christmas tradition and activity to fit into the thirty days between Thanksgiving and Christmas? We know such a packing job is impossible, but every year we keep trying anyway.

In the helter-skelter, we end up squishing some lovely items and leaving others out altogether. Are we happy about that? Not really. But come next December, we start jamming days and nights once again.

We would all do well to sit down on Thanksgiving night, after the turkey has been consumed and the football game has ended, and make a list of our Christmas traditions. *Between now and December 25, what are all the things our family wants to accomplish/enjoy/experience?* Everything from decorating the house to baking twelve dozen cookies to getting cards in the mail to singing in a church or community musical to reading *A Christmas Carol* aloud after supper to making and celebrating an Advent wreath to. . .

By the time we reach the bottom of the second page, we will be appropriately discouraged. So many good things, so little time . . .

Next step: Go back over the list and put a "C" alongside all activities that contain some kind of overt Christian principle. Which of these things will enhance the true meaning of Christmas for us and our children? Which are good, decent things to do, but expendable?

In light of the time crunch, start making choices based on the following Scripture: "Don't copy the behaviors and customs of this world, but be a new and different person with a fresh newness in all you do and think. Then you will learn from your own experience how his ways will really satisfy you" (Rom. 12:2, TLB). The Phillips translation says, "Don't let the world around you squeeze you into its mold.''

In December, that takes work! Effort! Not only we but also our children are bombarded by expectations from the past plus commercialism in the present. Everybody else has a thousand ideas about how to fill up our time. That is why we parents must get the jump on them by *choosing* our holiday activities (not being stampeded into them) and then presenting them positively to our children.

From Grasping to Giving

How do we make our homes into islands of sharing in the ocean of gimme?

We can cut down on the mountains of presents. We can lower our children's expectations by saying early in the month, ''Joey, you'll be receiving one large gift from us this year and two or three little things in your stocking.'' This really helps a child know there is a boundary. It stops the fantasizing about outlandish numbers of gifts.

We can refrain from displaying all the wrapped presents immediately upon purchase. All the mounds of glitter in front of kids' eyes for days on end only make them high. Families that bring *nothing* out of the closet until Christmas Eve perhaps have a point.

Or we can step out of the tradition and settle on one major gift for the family as a whole—either an item (new or used piano? home computer?) or an experience (a trip together?).

We can draw names within the family and then each prepare a secret *no-cost* gift to be presented separate from the others. (In our family, we exchange these right after dinner on Christmas Eve, and they generate tremendous warmth and appreciation. Examples: a homemade picture collage, ''coupons'' for free snow shoveling, a parent's childhood treasure to pass on to the next generation, a made-up game.)

We can prepare a small box with a gift-wrapped lid to be placed in front of the créche as a ''gift for Jesus.'' Each family member is to put money into the box at various times throughout December, so that on Christmas Eve the whole amount can be taken to church. Some churches even highlight a "gift for Jesus" offering and encourage families to bring these wrapped boxes of cash to lay on the altar; you might suggest such an idea in your church.

Alternate uses: Put the money toward a piece of equipment the church needs. Or take it to a Salvation Army "kettle" on the street, or give it to some other ministry to the needy, in the spirit of Matthew 25:40 ". . .Whatever you did for one of the least of these brothers of mine, you did for me."

In our home, this is the first gift ever set out; it finds its place in front of the lighted manger scene in our family room before any other presents are displayed. For young children, this tangible present does much to nail down whose birthday it really is on December 25.

The Advent Wreath

As explained in chapter one, our whole experiment with a Home Together Night was birthed during Advent. Our son was five, our daughters were two-and-a-half—would this work? Could we pull off anything meaningful?

Something about the soft atmosphere of candlelight in the dining room, the soft guitar chords, and the singing of carols enraptured the children. We kept the wreath time very brief so they would look forward to it next week. That first year we used the traditional purple and pink candles, with the large white one in the middle reserved for Christmas Day.

Through the years, we have changed the colors. Some years we've used a simple styrofoam ring as the base; eventually we bought a wrought-iron wreath. One year we followed a booklet that named the four candles *prophecy, Bethlehem, shepherds,* and *angels*—all quite concrete words for little ones. Another booklet led us toward *promise, light, love,* and *hope.*

One year we forgot about devotional guides and made up our

own theme: God's love for *all* the people of the world. The candles were red, yellow, black, and white. We read stories about Christians in other lands and then followed up with at least two planned family activities to help those of other skin colors (Vietnamese and Ethiopian refugee families we knew).

In 1983 we centered on the idea of *giving:*

Week 1: God's gift to us in sending Jesus.
Week 2: Being content with our gifts (we read aloud a magazine story about a person's most memorable Christmas when he *didn't* get the gift of his dreams).
Week 3: Giving to the needy or ill.
Week 4: Jesus' ultimate gift to us—eternal life.

In 1984, with our children getting still older, we turned the entire month into a search for Old Testament hints about the coming of Christ. The first night, Dean said, "When you read a Hardy Boys book or some other mystery, you're always guessing whether something has special importance or not. That's the way it is in the Old Testament, too. God was always dropping little clues about the future and then watching to see whether anybody would notice. Some of his clues are *really* obscure, so you'll have to be sharp."

We then took turns being Cluemaster of the Week (for which you got to wear a Sherlock Holmes-type hat). The Cluemaster got to use matches to light the candles, pass out one clue to each member of the family, call on each person in turn to read, guide the discussion of which lines in the reading had special significance about the Messiah's coming, then choose a closing carol for all to sing, and finally snuff out the candle flames. Big honor!

Here's the collection of clues:

1. Genesis 3:14-15
2. Genesis 22:15-18; 26:4-5
3. Genesis 49:1-2, 8-12
4. Deuteronomy 18:15.
5. 1 Chronicles 17:3-4, 11-14
6. Psalm 2
7. Psalm 110:1-4
8. Psalm 118:22-26
9. Psalm 132:11-13, 17-18
10. Isaiah 7:13-14

11. Isaiah 9:1-3, 6-7
12. Isaiah 11:1-6
13. Isaiah 42:1-4
14. Isaiah 49:1-6
15. Isaiah 59:20
16. Isaiah 61:1-3
17. Jeremiah 23:5-6
18. Jeremiah 33:14-17
19. Ezekiel 34:20-24
20. Daniel 9:20-26
21. Micah 5:2-5a
22. Haggai 2:6-9
23. Zechariah 3:8-9
24. Zechariah 6:12-13
25. Malachi 3:1-4

Christian bookstores have any number of resources for Advent wreath celebrations. They also usually stock craft/activity books and Advent calendars that focus on the Nativity instead of the old man from up north.

Other Ways to Major on the Majors

A special heritage can be found by memorizing the Christmas story—Luke 2:1-20 (or just 7-16)—as a family. You start by parceling out sections: Dad and Sarah take on four verses, while Mom and Tim take the next four, and so forth. Working in pairs helps lighten the load of effort that memorization requires.

There must be a goal, of course: to recite the passage for the relatives on Christmas Eve or Christmas morning, just before the gift opening. This becomes a special moment as parent and child together present the truth about Christmas.

As the years go by, of course, everybody ends up learning the entire passage, mostly from listening to the others. Once Luke is mastered, you can move on to Matthew 2:1-12, the arrival of the Magi.

Another option: memorize the verses of a relatively unfamiliar Christmas carol, one stanza each week. This will set you up for some family caroling, perhaps to neighbors' homes, shut-ins you know, teachers from school or church. It is, in fact, an entirely valid and welcomed way to share your faith with non-Christians. You don't have to get some large group together to carol; just do it yourself!

One year we allowed the children each to hold a lighted candle as we surprised people by standing in their darkened front yards singing about Jesus. We then left a small gift we'd made earlier in the evening: half a dozen homemade cookies in a plastic bag, tucked inside a homemade pouch (see drawing, below). We simply took pairs of large Christmas cards from the year before, cut off the backs, matched up the fronts in one hand, punched holes around three sides, and strung them together with yarn, allowing a yarn handle at the top.

Outdoor decorations are an obvious way to reflect the real center of Christmas. Kids love to nail things together—why not a star-shaped frame on which to string lights? It can then be hung from a window frame, garage, or apartment balcony. This is really easier than you might think.

After creating a star one year, we added the lighted store-bought figures of Mary, Joseph, and the baby Jesus the next. The year after that we nailed together scraps of 2x4's and 1x6's to make a rustic stable about three feet high. We "borrow" some straw each year from friends who have a mini-farm, and our outdoor display is now complete—(unless we get inspired to add recorded music or something!). It has been fun to let the children plan, design, and build these things, all for the purpose of presenting a witness to passersby.

Do you know a refugee family? Do you know someone struggling financially? While there are many fine programs at Christmastime to aid people, your children will get the point much more powerfully—and escape the me-me-me syndrome at least temporarily—if you reach out with food and clothing and gifts *directly*, not just by writing a check to a fund.

You might even leave a bag of toys and goodies anonymously. You'll want to talk together about your feelings as you drive home afterward.

Or you might make a cassette tape for someone overseas or a lonely relative out of state.

At some point in December, *make sure* you take time for some kind of personal outreach. Christmas is not complete without it.

Here are additional ideas to consider. Our creative Lord will give you thoughts of your own as well on ways to major on the majors this time of year.

- Prepare a birthday cake for Jesus as the centerpiece of your Christmas table.
- Give your church a *gift of time*—cleaning, stuffing bulletins, whatever.
- Have a family "program" on Christmas Eve or sometime, each member planning a song, a drawing, a poem, a Scripture—and keeping it a surprise until called upon.
- Visit a nursing home on Christmas afternoon. Take along little favors to pass out. This is an especially lonely time for those few who have *not* been picked up for the day.
- Invite a foreign student or a single person to Christmas dinner.
- Buy or borrow the Christmas story in flannelgraph figures,

and have neighborhood children over for a party, using the story as the main feature. Your kids may want to practice ahead of time and do the presentation.

- Do something totally unexpected for a neighbor—shovel the snow from his or her driveway or parking place while he or she is at work, for example.
- At dinner each evening, pray for those whose Christmas cards arrived in your mailbox today.
- Create a "Party in a Package"—hot chocolate mix, cookies, napkins, cups, placemats—and then go enjoy it with some surprised family you know.
- Give a wrapped-up "gift of time" (coupon) to each member of your family.
- Fight for time to read quality Christmas books with your children. You read a page or chapter, then they read, then you.
- Tape up a length of shelving paper on a wall and encourage children to draw the Christmas story, using markers, Christ-centered stencils, and Christmas cards.
- Invite your child's Sunday school teacher over for a meal or dessert.
- Play Christmas records every day. Your family will learn the carols without even trying.
- Study the Christmas customs of a country where missionaries you know are living. Pattern your holiday after theirs if you can. Then write and tell them how it went.
- Encourage the editor of your local paper to run an essay contest for kids on "The True Meaning of Christmas."
- Curl up with popcorn and watch any good TV specials about Christmas. One Charlie Brown version ends with Linus doing a word-for-word recitation of Luke 2.

The Big Moment

Finally, the long-awaited time comes (in some families, Christmas Eve; in others, Christmas morning). Children's pulse rates soar as they approach the hour of bliss.

Must it be a binge of self-gratification? In Dean's earlier book, *How to Really Love Your Wife*, the following account of a stressful evening back in 1976 appears:

> Grace's parents were with us for the traditional Scandinavian Christmas Eve dinner, and as we opened their gifts afterward, the kids were very wound up and the whole scene seemed more like bedlam than anything else. What blew my fuse was when Nathan (then age four), having torn through several nice presents in less than fifteen minutes, looked up and whined, "Is that all I get?"
>
> I reprimanded him, apologized to his grandparents, and made a silent resolution that Gift Time No. 2, scheduled for the next morning, would be different. Late that night, after everything had calmed down and the wrappings and ribbons had been squashed into the trash can, I went to the basement and got six cardboard boxes. I sorted out the remaining gifts as follows:
>
> - Gifts *from* Nathan
> - Gifts *from* Rhonda
> - Gifts *from* Tricia
> - Gifts *from* Mom and Dad
> - Gifts *from* Grandma and Grandpa Merrill
> - Gifts *from* our friends
>
> The next morning when everyone got up, the boxes with signs attached were sitting on a high table. I explained that each of us would take turns getting a gift from his box and *giving* it to someone else in the room, and that we'd all watch to see what had been given before going on to the next gift. By shifting the spotlight from getting to giving, I hoped to restore some of the meaning we'd lost.
>
> It worked. Even the twins at twenty-one months of age seemed to catch the idea as they toddled around placing gifts in other people's hands. Since my parents weren't present, the children were allowed to make their presentations too. The whole experience was quieter, not at all frenzied, and reflected the symbolism of God giving us his Son. When, later in the day, I asked Nathan, "What did you *give* for Christmas?" he was able to list a number of things, and the pride that showed on his face told me he was pleased.

That system has now worked for a dozen years and has become standard procedure throughout our extended family. It has revolutionized gift-opening time into something precious, with hands reaching out rather than pulling inward. Now that the children are older, we don't go to the bother of using large boxes. We simply pass out the gifts to their *givers* rather than receivers; then we go around the circle as many times as necessary making presentations. When someone runs out of personal gifts to present, he or she begins making proxy presentations using the gifts that arrived by mail.

The kids often kneel alongside the person opening a gift, and it's a moment of special closeness.

Early Milestones: Birthdays

By the time children reach the grade-school years, they are starting to amass a personal history. The memory bank is building. They can look back to "when I was little" and feel proud about their growing maturity.

We parents may as well seize the opportunity, especially at birthday times, to reinforce that concept. "You're getting bigger; you're growing up. You're becoming your own person."

To make all this visual, give the child a long strip of drawing paper and some help to create "My Life So Far"—a time line. Mark off the years, write in the date of birth on the far left, and then ask, "What else do you remember? What have been the highlights of your life to this point?"

Likely entries:

"First real bed" (no more crib)
"First bike"
"First bike accident"
"Summer trip to ______________"
"Preschool"
"Kindergarten, Mrs. ______" "Grade 1, Mrs. ______"
"T-ball" or "soccer season"

Your children may want to embellish their time lines with drawings of various events; the charts may end up quite colorful by the time you tape them to a wall. Then you can say: "Do you know what? You're making the same journey Jesus made when he was growing up. That's what the Bible tells about in Luke 2:52—'And Jesus grew in wisdom and stature, and in favor with God and men.' Let's make an extra strip to go above our time lines and write the verse on it."

By the time you finish this addition, your children will have the verse memorized.

The year our twins turned eight, Dean took each of them to a quiet bedroom before the festive dinner and said, "Let's think a minute about how the Lord has helped you grow this far. In a little while, after we eat, I'm going to call on you to stand up and say, 'During my first eight years, the Lord has helped me to . . .' Let's write a list of things you can tell about."

This gave the opportunity for each girl not only to recount answers to prayer and problems she had conquered but also to give a "mini-testimonial" about her personal decision to follow Christ (made a year or two previous). Putting these important matters into words in front of one's family and grandparents was stretching in itself, reinforcing awareness and determination to "grow in the grace and knowledge of our Lord and Savior Jesus Christ" (2 Pet. 3:18).

I Am a Possibility: Honor Nights

In a world of giants, it is sometimes hard for dwarfs to think highly of themselves. And we grown-up giants are often too busy, too self-impressed, to remember what it was like as one of the little people.

The writer who has taught us most about remembering this is Wayne Rickerson. Throughout his books on family life, he is constantly calling parents to affirm, stroke, and elevate the fragile personalities of children. Psychological terms such as *self-worth, self-esteem, self-acceptance,* and *a good self-image* may come to sound effete after a while, but they describe a very real need in the life of every God-made boy and girl.

Cockiness? No. Boastfulness? No. But good, comfortable feelings of value—yes. That's why the Gaithers wrote the children's song "I Am a Promise." We must help our offspring believe that every week.

How? By searching with them for their particular field for excelling, be it a sport, an instrument, or something else. By guarding against an overload of correction in any one day, mixing in plenty of "I still like you" messages and actions. By taking time to listen attentively. As someone with a great measure of wisdom has said, "Love is giving a person your undivided attention." Do we love our children?

Rickerson talks in his book *Getting Your Family Together* (Regal) about the Honor Night concept, and at our house, we're great believers in its value. One child is selected for special limelight throughout the evening—which isn't his or her birthday or anything else, just a selected time each year when the family zeroes in and says, "We think you're great!"

Let's say it's Rhonda Night. When she was younger, she got to select the main course of the meal. (Now she not only chooses the menu but also goes shopping with Mom for the necessary groceries and then prepares the food.)

The table centerpiece one year was a display of her favorite things: Cabbage Patch doll, flute, her copy of *Charlotte's Web*, a piece of beloved jewelry. Once we sat down to eat, a homemade star with glitter was pinned on her. She beamed.

After the meal, she sits on a chair in the middle of the room for a "press conference." The rest of the family take turns asking things such as "What's your favorite subject in school?" "What has been a happy moment in the last couple of weeks?" and "What is your favorite book/color/hobby?" We actually learn some things we didn't know.

We may bring out her baby remembrance book and read some significant parts. We may discuss how her name was chosen and what it means, or tell about her birth—the miracle of her survival in spite of being born six weeks early and having severe breathing distress the first couple of days. We may show slides from the first year of her life. For each of the three children, we have shown slides of their dedication at church and played the tape recording of the pastor's prayer and comments. We share our spiritual commitment, made that day, to raise them in a godly home. They love hearing these things over and over.

Several years ago we made a compliment flower for Rhonda, with her name in the center and four construction paper petals, on which each of us wrote a word such as *loving* or *enthusiastic* or *talented* before gluing the pieces together. The flower was then taped to her bedroom wall, where it stayed for weeks, sending out its encouragement. (For Nathan, the art was switched to a basketball court with compliments written on basketballs headed for the hoop.)

We may choose a special verse of Scripture that expresses our feelings about this child (2 Cor. 7:16, for example) and turn it into a puzzle by writing one word on the bottom of each nut cup or a piece of paper under each placemat. Once the meal is over, the children try to assemble the verse in proper order. By that time, they've virtually memorized it.

Grace once planned our Circle Time around Psalm 139:13-18, where David praises God for the wonder of being created in his mother's womb. "God planned and shaped you inside of me, before you were ever born," Grace said, "and each day is a little more of his plan for your life." Then came a special prayer of thanks for Rhonda and requests for guidance in the future.

More recently, we've asked the child to select a favorite Bible story, read it to us, and lead a discussion based on questions he or she has written. Too much for a grade schooler to attempt? Not really, especially when the pattern of a Circle Time is well established.

The finale of the evening is for the child of honor to choose a game for everyone to play.

This has become an annual event for each of the three children over the years, and it never seems to wear out. (Some families might want to schedule this kind of evening on the child's spiritual birthday, the anniversary of when a commitment to follow Christ was made.)

The same kind of event works well with Mom or Dad. Mother's Day and Father's Day are good times of the year to help children focus on their parents as special people. The same format, with interviews, photos of the past, a compliment device, and so forth, can be used.

Beyond these special occasions, there are scores of ways to keep building up our children, boosting their morale:

- Draw names out of a bowl and write complimentary poems about each other.
- Have each person write the letters of his or her first name vertically on a piece of paper. Then turn the papers over, shuffle them, and pass them out again. Each person writes something positive about the person whose name appears.

Example:

Tall
Really plays violin well
Is bouncy!
Clever in creative writing
Is a Christian
Artistic

Or you can circulate the papers round-robin style, adding a positive note to the next line of each paper as it comes your way.

- Make a compliment chart and pass it around collecting entries. (This kind of activity works best while some other project is underway.) Dad fills in a short compliment in each box on the top row except his own, then passes the chart on to Nathan, and so forth. When you're finished, post it on the refrigerator. It's guaranteed to dispel a week of miscellaneous blues.
- During dinner: Say something nice to the person on your right, not *about* them, but *to* them—for example, "I like the way you draw."

It's this kind of reinforcement that makes a Home Together Night sparkle. It's the reason we don't allow interruptions, telephone calls, and all the rest. The message both spoken and unspoken is "You are special. You are valuable. You are a treasure."

What Value Valentine's Day?

February 14 can be more than childish frivolity—if we have eyes to see its potential. What a natural time to highlight the theme of love at home!

In so doing, of course, we switch the subject from romantic puppy love to genuine caring and affection—but the kids hardly notice. An example: One year we piled the table with ribbon, construction paper, Elmer's glue, doilies, and markers to make old-fashioned valentine cards for elderly neighbors of Grace's parents, who lived in a nearby retirement complex. These were people who would get precious few valentines.

The fact that Mom and Dad joined the kids in making these cards produced its own special warmth.

The responses from the senior citizens, as you might well imagine, were joyous and deeply felt. One gentleman widower has sent our children valentines and birthday cards every year since!

Actually, it's not necessary that your family know the recipients of your cards. You can use a list of elderly church members and simply inscribe a message that says, "Just wanting to share God's love with you on Valentine's Day. From the Jones family at Riverdale Church."

Meanwhile, this holiday is an excellent time to define true love according to the Scripture. One year we took a large red piece of construction paper, cut it into the shape of a heart, and wrote *LOVE* in the center with a marker. Then we took turns adding the descriptions of love we heard as Nathan read 1 Corinthians 13 aloud: *patient, loyal, doesn't hold grudges, never jealous, doesn't demand its own way, kind, the greatest,* and so forth. These were spread randomly at all angles around the heart.

Next we drew jigsaw lines between the various words. The heart was then passed around with a pair of scissors to be cut apart. You'd be surprised at how hard it was to reassemble, even for parents! We closed by praying together for these qualities of love to grow in each of our lives.

The puzzle remained a fun activity for the kids and their friends over several days, its message lingering to remind them of a choice truth of God's Word.

The legend of St. Valentinus is another useful tool to give this day meaning. There really was such a man, you know—a Roman priest who was imprisoned during the reign of Claudius II (A.D. 268-270) for helping persecuted Christians.

While awaiting his execution, Valentinus became friends with the jailor's blind daughter. In fact, we are told that after he prayed for her, she regained her sight. The night before his death, he wrote her a farewell message to say he would remember her throughout all eternity. He signed it, "From your Valentine."

This friendship between a Christian leader and a child (assuming the story is reliable) was of course incorporated later into the pagan Roman festival of Lupercalia, which took place in mid-February for the benefit of lovers. (Similar mixing and revising occurred with Christmas, Easter, and Halloween at various stages of history.) But the original story is worth retelling on February 14.

The above festivities take place at our house following one of Grace's "red meals"—a menu chosen on the basis of color: spaghetti or pizza, a red heart-shaped Jell-O mold, cherry drink, and a dessert of strawberry sundaes or else a strawberry-frosted cake (again, in a heart shape, cut from a thirteen by nine cake) or cookies. Baking has often included the children as junior chefs after school.

If Home Together Night falls on February 14 and your kids come home from school with bagfuls of valentines, these can become a colorful table decoration. Let the children arrange the cards all over a white or red paper table covering; then cover the collage with clear plastic. Or at least run a strip of cards down the center of the table. Some of them usually have cute riddles to spice the suppertime conversation.

Even the family members can be required to don something red before being allowed to sit down and eat!

Outrunning the Easter Bunny

The Easter rabbit is fast at work each spring to monopolize children's attention, interest, and time. We parents often tend to let him dominate; we even chip in an egg hunt, a few chocolate bunnies, and hope that Easter Sunday morning's church service will supply the spiritual part.

For this most important Christian holiday of the year, however, that is not enough. Just as with Advent, the key lies in *planning ahead*. To keep Holy Week from slipping up, choose a good book well in advance to read aloud after evening meals (or whenever). Here are some of our favorites:

Vinegar Boy by Alberta Hawse (Moody)—a fiction story of a badly birthmarked boy in the first century who has a dramatic encounter with Christ on the cross.

The Lion, the Witch and the Wardrobe by C.S. Lewis (Macmillan)—the popular and powerful fantasy that climaxes with Aslan the Lion's return to life. Its winter-to-spring context fits the Lenten season beautifully.

Easter Bunny, Are You for Real? by Harold Myra (Nelson) does a good job of separating myth from fact.

Primary-age children enjoy hearing (or getting to read aloud themselves) from a Bible storybook such as *Jesus, the Friend of Children* (David C. Cook), with its stirring pictures of the Triumphal Entry, the Last Supper, the garden of Gethsemane, Golgotha, and the empty tomb.

Be sure to allow time for spontaneous conversation about what you're reading.

If you peruse the TV or movie listings, you'll find that even the media get a little religious at Easter time. Most likely you'll spot a good film for the family: *Jesus, Jesus of Nazareth, The Prodigal,*

Chariots of Fire, or *The Lion, the Witch and the Wardrobe*, to name just a few. More than once we've curled up together as a family in pajamas with popcorn to watch a two-hour TV movie that has driven home the Crucifixion in a powerful way.

(A good follow-up activity: write letters to the advertisers thanking them for sponsoring the program. Let them know how you appreciate their provision of good, wholesome material. This does more good than writing the station or network; *advertisers* call the shots in this industry.)

The younger actors in the family may want to get up and perform themselves; the Palm Sunday story is a natural. Provide them with real palm branches from a florist to heighten the drama. (And buy enough extras for your children to take to their classes on Sunday.) Or, the women's surprising discovery at the empty tomb is another great script for playacting at home.

Banners make an excellent pre-Easter activity. Make one for your living room or family room during the season, or a small one for each child's bedroom, or as gifts to your dinner guests.

Good Friday is normally a school holiday, and often the adults are off work as well. If so, try having a Galilean breakfast—outdoors if possible—with broiled fish, eggs, juice, and bread (or hot cross buns). Invite a neighbor family to join you, and finish by reading John 21 together to show the source of your ideas. (Easter morning is too busy for all of this, but the free Friday is just right.)

Talk together about the name *Good Friday.* Does it fit? Should the day be called Dark Friday instead? Why not?

If your church or community has a Good Friday service, take time to attend it as a family. If it's a noon-to-three service built around the seven last sayings of Christ on the cross, you'll probably want to go for just part of the time—but before you do, write a list of the seven phrases. You and the children will have to consult all four gospels to find them, which will be a good research hunt. Then note which phrase is being featured at the point you enter the service.

Or if you stay home, write personal notes to Jesus (i.e., prayers) thanking him for suffering for you. Once they're written, perhaps your children would like to copy theirs into the flyleaf of their Bibles, adding the date. This can be a sobering way to encounter the death of Christ on our behalf.

Above all, don't make the mistake of letting Good Friday come and go as just another ordinary day.

With these preparations, Easter itself becomes all the more thrilling. You can decorate eggs with sayings such as "He Lives," "Jesus Is Alive," "Jesus Rose," "He Died for Me," or drawings of the cross or the empty tomb. Simply write with crayons on the hard-boiled eggs before dipping them into the color solution. The crayon marking resists the dye and stands out in contrast.

You may want to retell the Easter story to visiting relatives or neighbor children using pantomime, puppets, flannel-graph pictures, or costumes.

As at Thanksgiving, you can tuck special verses about the risen Christ inside your table place cards and pass a Bible around after Easter dinner. Older children can help select these.

One year we memorized as a family the first stanza of the gospel song "He Lives," another year "Up from the Grave He Arose." This allowed the children to sing vigorously at church every time those songs were announced.

The point of all the above suggestions: to make the most out of what is a fundamentally Christian celebration. Just as we seek to point children to the babe in the manger, we must also make a conscious effort to immerse them in the wonder of Easter.

Of Seeds and Weeds: Spring

Children are naturally fascinated with the planting-growing process; that's why nearly every kindergartner in the country starts sunflowers or beans in paper cups. Kids are amazed at how the tiny little round thing turns into a stem with leaves and a flower on top. They watch excitedly as parents plant vegetable or flower gardens at home each spring.

So why not take advantage of this natural curiosity to make Jesus' parable of the sower come alive?

The approach is easy enough. You simply say, "It's about time we got started with our garden this year. The first thing we're going to do is read a story Jesus told about planting seeds." Proceed with Mark 4:1-9.

Then say, "Let's each go find a spot around our yard or close by that's like Jesus described. Who wants to find a hard path? A rocky place? A place full of weeds and thorns? A patch of good soil? Let's go! Meet back here as soon as you pick your spot."

Once everyone returns, take a tour together, led first by the finder of the hard path, then the finder of the rocky place, and so forth. At each stop, say, "Jesus said this had something to do with how people respond to the Word of God. He also said some people wouldn't get his point at all—but some would. What do you think *this* place stands for?" Reopen your Bible and draw upon verses 13-20 (Jesus' explanation) as needed. (This will depend on whether your children have already had this story in Sunday school or not. Even if they have, the review here in the open air is good.)

Eventually, of course, you wind up at the garden plot—good soil ready to receive the seed and do something with it. Say something like "I sure hope *our* family is like this kind of soil: that we hear God's message and really put it to use in our lives."

Then bring out the seed packets and proceed with an all-family planting session. Or you might want to plant seeds in all the spots and watch to see if the seeds in the hard or rocky places grow.

Good News for the World: Missions

One of our deepest desires is for our children to be "world Christians"—those who know their faith wasn't invented in the U.S.A. The spiritual link with brothers and sisters on other continents is not only a duty to maintain but also an enrichment to enjoy. Our lives were forever changed by traveling overseas with youth music teams during college days, and we're determined to pass along this global view of God's kingdom to the next generation.

Many Christian parents share this burden, we know. Here are some ways and means.

If you're part of a church that has an annual or semiannual missions emphasis, don't make the church do all the work!

Does a visiting speaker need housing or a meal? Your children's minds and imaginations will be tremendously stretched as they rub elbows with a "real live missionary," perhaps even giving up their bedroom for a night on the couch in a sleeping bag (they've been begging you for that anyway, right?). As they see and hear someone up close who serves God in a foreign culture, the idea of a career in missions for *them* may take its first root.

If your church solicits special pledges or "faith promises" to the missions fund, encourage your child to put his or her own name on a dotted line, separate from yours. The amount may be small, but the act is significant. (Yes, this makes extra bookkeeping for the church, but it will pay off in years to come when the habit of missions giving is firmly entrenched.)

Help your children understand what's at stake here: the spread of the gospel to countries very different from theirs. Assist them week by week in preparing their gifts, and pray together from time to time on Sunday morning (perhaps at the breakfast table), asking God to bless and multiply your gifts.

One year our church requested families to make large banners of a specified size to brighten the sanctuary with the theme "Lord of All." We spent three Home Together Nights getting ours ready (one to brainstorm the design and purchase the materials, two to create the finished product). It included a crown at the top with "Lord of All" in bright letters, then shapes of various countries (traced from an atlas) appliquéd to the background, with miniature flags extending from the shapes.

How exciting it was to see the unique ideas of each family that participated! The mood for the week was enthusiastic. In subsequent years, new themes have been announced and carried out. (This might be a good idea to suggest to your church's missions committee.)

The actual family night of such a week can feature an international meal. Our menu over the years has ranged from simple tacos to full-scale Indian curry with all the fiery condiments (prepared by our guests for the night, an Indian family in our church). As we ate, they told us about customs in their country, how their families had become Christian, and gave us a sampling of conversation in Tamil. After dessert, we saw slides of their wedding—an arranged marriage.

Whether you know an international family to invite or not, you can enhance the atmosphere by playing records from other lands (check your local library) and bringing out whatever foreign mementos, toys, and articles of clothing you have or can borrow from friends.

Some mission organizations have ready-made projects that fit families. Once we packed up a box of extra Bibles around the house, just sitting on shelves, and sent them to the World Home Bible League (South Holland, Illinois), which had announced it could put them to good use.

On several occasions we've purchased a box of paperback New Testaments from Bibles for the World (Box 805, Wheaton, IL 60187) to be mailed overseas. This organization specializes in mailing the Scriptures unsolicited to addresses gathered from the telephone books of the world. What most North Americans don't realize is that in many other countries, only the educated, literate class have telephones—the very people who can be reached for Christ by a copy of the Scriptures in their language. The kits include corrugated wrappers and pre-typed address labels.

Our part is to wrap the Testaments, affix the labels, pray over the finished stack that God will speak to the recipients through this medium, and then take the parcels to the post office. This hands-on experience has made missions live for our children.

We got infinitely more involved the winter our church sponsored a Vietnamese refugee family. It was a fascinating, baffling, exhilarating, exasperating (at times) experience for us all to relate to five non-English speakers who had fled North Vietnam to Hong Kong and then to this country. Our children watched us find an apartment for them, scavenge furniture from all our friends, taxi the family here and there. . .and the kids themselves had to learn how to communicate with nods and smiles, how to be gracious when served tea and rice *every* visit to their place, no matter how brief or at what hour. They grappled with finding Christmas presents for the Vietnamese children that required no reading but would still be age-appropriate.

They also sat on the floor and listened as Bibles were read, first in Cantonese, then in English. They silently affirmed the prayers in both languages. They rejoiced with us the night the parents were baptized after deciding to follow Christ.

In time the family grew weary of Illinois winters and relocated to San Jose. But we have stayed in touch throughout the years. We shall always be grateful for this intense plunge into the task of cross-cultural missions.

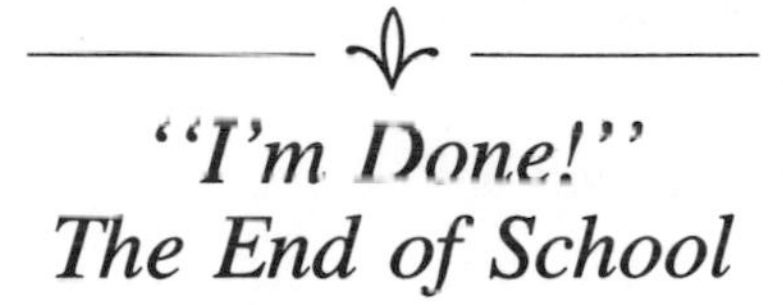

"I'm Done!" The End of School

Isn't it a great feeling to *finish* something? Anything!

Kids feel the same way. Whether they are straight-A students or marginal strugglers, they look forward to finishing their many projects, cleaning out their desks, and heading for summertime. It's only appropriate for parents to rejoice with them the next family night.

If you can find *anything* to praise on the report card—*do it!* Make sure your child doesn't become one of those adults (there seem to be thousands of them these days) who still carry scars from striving mightily for a B in some course, winding up with a B *minus*, and having their father grunt, "How come you didn't get an A?"

We happen to believe that school is the child's employment; it's his or her major work for these years. That means it deserves respect. Although we know many parents will disagree with us, we believe our children's work is worthy of the same kind of compensation adults get: *cash*. It's our way of saying, "We know school is tough sometimes and you really have to bear down. You worked hard; now here's your reward."

Thus, at each report card time, we pay lucratively according to a scale: for example, each A gets a dollar, each B fifty cents. We've dreamed up a variety of incremental payments for plus marks or whatever, depending on the school's grading system. And we give double weight to behavior or "citizenship" grades, to show that no matter what happens academically, Mom and Dad are *very* interested in how you conduct yourself at school.

The above paragraphs should not be taken to mean that we drive our children to make the honor roll or else. Our standard is rather expressed in the saying, "All we want is your best." For some children, a C may be their best. If so, reward it lavishly. Simply adjust your pay scale.

The presentation is as much of a big deal at our house as the money itself. At times we've had a mock ceremony a la the Emmy Awards ("And *now*, ladies and gentlemen—may I have the envelope for Tricia Merrill, please!") Kids shiver with glee as they are called up to receive their crisp, fresh-from-the-bank greenbacks.

At other times, we sneak the money under their overturned plates at dinner. This reflects a tradition in the Merrill family from way back: whenever you come to the table for a meal and your plate or bowl is upside down, it means a surprise is underneath and you have to wait until after the prayer to turn it over.

Some families, we realize, have wide variations between siblings when it comes to grades. If competitive feelings run high, it may be wise to present each child's reward in private.

When a son or daughter completes elementary school or junior high, it's probably worth an even greater splash, perhaps a dinner out at a fancy restaurant and/or a wrapped-up gift.

Prayers at all these occasions should reflect a thankfulness to God for his help, for giving the child a mind to develop, for strength to overcome the hard times this past school year, and for the growing bank of knowledge and maturity. A special song to sing, if you know it, is the modern spiritual "We've Come This Far by Faith."

Summer: Ordeal or Opportunity?

Summertime with children can be an ordeal—weeks of helter-skelter that leave parents drained and counting the days till school resumes. Or it can be a great opportunity—a privilege to have the major input to our children once again. Two things make the difference:

Attitude. If we consciously pray about gaining a positive, expectant attitude toward June, July, and August, God will give it to us.

Planning. This is an old theme song of ours, but it needs replaying here. "Winging it" simply won't work. Sit down early in May to read Scripture, pray, and think about each individual child under your roof. What does he need most this summer? What are her strengths to be enhanced? What would God most want you to accomplish by Labor Day? Jot notes. Ponder. Meditate.

In an hour or two, direction will emerge specifically tailored to *your* family members. You'll get a focus on where you're headed spiritually with the children, what practical things need to be worked on, whether Karen should or shouldn't take summer band, whether everyone belongs in swimming lessons, or whether Jeff needs a break from schedule demands. . . . How do your vacation plans fit into all this? Or should you change them? Should you maybe do a "vacation at home" this year?

Both the major events and the everyday things will come to light and begin to synchronize. Believe us: this works, and it's exciting to go into summer with a plan.

The Preview

On a family night shortly before school lets out, share what you've come up with. Give some "commercials" for the weeks ahead. Kids, like adults, do better when the future is not entirely a void before them.

Also, discuss these questions:

"What would *you* like to do this summer just for fun?"

"What would you like to *learn* this summer?"

Depending on their ages, they may have some excellent vacation input—things you hadn't thought about. Try not to ridicule the impractical or extravagant suggestions; just pass over them with a "We'll see." Let the children help with travel research, either at a library or by writing letters to tourist offices. If a boy or girl is interested, teach how to read a road map, plan a route, and calculate the mileage (good math drill!).

Along with the above, mix in the summer house rules and boundaries—what house-yard-garden work will be expected now that kids have more free time, what the new (later) bedtimes will be now that school is ending, what notice Mom expects before friends are invited over to play—plus a reinforcement of the fact that Mom or Dad must *always* know where you are, twenty-four hours a day. That's just non-negotiable.

On Ordinary Days

Since the children are no longer memorizing things for school, summer is prime time for Scripture memorization. This may be the time to initiate individual file boxes (see "The Secret of Scripture Memory" elsewhere in this book for details). But plan some kind of memorizing strategy for the family.

The last couple of summers we've challenged our children to master a longer passage: an entire psalm or other classic text, such as Philippians 2:5-16, James 1:1-12, John 14, or a chapter of the Sermon on the Mount (Matt. 5-7). We announced a financial reward. (Is this wrong? We don't think so, any more than a smile, a compliment, or a free trip to camp is wrong; they're all extrinsic motivators to woo a child along until he or she reaches the maturity of choosing to memorize Scripture for intrinsic reasons. Even a lot of adults aren't *that* mature!)

In our case, we found the texts were recited and the prizes claimed before the end of June. Children this age have inkblotter brains that are more than equal to mountainous-sounding tasks. They love the challenge, followed by the satisfaction of being able to recite a whole section of God's Word.

Summertime is also the year's best opportunity to encourage a child's daily time with the Lord alone. Be sure to allow a block of time for this in every day's schedule, preferably in the morning. (It certainly beats cartoons and game shows.) Let them sometimes observe *you* sitting down with your Bible as a healthy model; don't always do this before they're out of bed.

Some kids will take off on their own, deciding "I'm going to read the whole New Testament this summer." Others will need help getting started, or restarted. We had great success one year using an idea from Linda Dillow and Claudia Arp's book *Sanity in the Summertime* (Nelson) in which the whole family reads the thirty-one chapters of Proverbs throughout July, one chapter a day. There's no losing track of where you should be; the calendar tells you! Each child makes a thirty-one-page Proverbs notebook and on each page: (1) writes a favorite or important verse from the day's chapter and (2) illustrates how to live out a truth from that chapter by drawing a stick-figure picture. Sometimes at the bottom the child can add a verse reference he or she would like to memorize or a "Lord, help me. . ." prayer.

Did it work? Yes! Especially since we sat down with each child on Sunday to review the week's entries, compliment the pictures, and ask questions. Proverbs is chockfull of nitty-gritty advice about money, laziness, words, temptation, compassion for the poor, and staying out of fights. That was the year we had an extra child for six weeks—a boy from a troubled neighborhood of Northern Ireland, as part of a peacemaking program called the Irish Children's Fund—and for the first time in his life he learned that the holy black book had something practical to say to *him*. We will get letters from Keith, and they usually mention that his Bible reading continues.

Another enrichment: decorate a box with a slot in the top as a Bible Question Box. Invite kids to drop in anything they wonder about that relates to the Bible or Christian living. Then spend time answering their questions on a family night.

Do you want to prevent excessive television watching in the summer? Do you want to teach selectivity and discretion? One of the best ways we've found—and it doesn't call for long sermons or harangues—is the daily time quota. We told our children, "That box over there is not going to run our lives. It's not going to control *us*. We're going to control *it*. So each day, you look through the *TV Guide* and make your choices. We've decided that three half-hours a day is enough. As you use up your watching time, mark off your X's on this refrigerator chart.

	Sun.	Mon.	Tues.	Wed.	Thurs.	Fri.	Sat.
Cindy							
Jeff							

"This way, you will always know where you stand, and so will Mom and Dad. When you've made your three X's for the day, you're done! It's time to do something else."

The genius of this plan is that with only three available slots, kids make *conscious, careful* choices. In an odd sort of way, less quantity results in better quality; we seldom have had to veto a choice.

If someone's quota is used up but someone else is still watching, the first person is required to be in a different part of the house. This encourages creativity to do other things.

We found that during the first couple of weeks, our kids were very zealous to mark the chart and make sure they got their full share. Then, gradually, the X's became more spotty. They genuinely discovered better ways to use their time and tended to forget about the TV quotas. That was even more than we had hoped for in the beginning. (We did make one variance for the resident Cubs fan! On days with baseball telecasts, Nathan's quota was stretched to a game plus *one* other half-hour.)

We've always had a no-TV rule during meals at our house, and in the summer, Grace has made lunchtime into a special treat. Following the practice of Mary Lou and Joseph Bayly, friends of ours who always took parenting seriously, she reads aloud from a quality children's book while the kids eat. (It's a great way to preempt arguing over the peanut butter.) We experience something together day after day—another segment in the life of a hero of the faith or a good secular adventure. (And Mom even gets to avoid calories in the process!)

On the Road

The same practice is great once the family heads out on vacation. On one trip to Yellowstone and back, we read an abridged version of *Pilgrim's Progress* (one of those Christian classics we all intend to read to our children but don't always get it done). It was an excellent story for a *trip* because the principal character, Christian, is also on a journey through mountains, alleys, fields, and towns, headed for the Celestial City. One chapter even spawned a lively discussion about death. Meanwhile, the miles clicked off unnoticed.

Group devotions are also a prime possibility in the car, as different family members take turns reading a Scripture passage for the day, followed by prayer. You can also memorize a verse together. On the same trip to Wyoming, we came in our reading to the familiar Philippians 4:13 ("I can do everything through him who gives me strength") and began talking about its context: "being content in any and every situation, whether well fed or hungry, whether living in plenty or in want" (v. 12).

Paul wrote this paragraph from jail. What about us? What are the situations in which *we* must ask Christ to strengthen us and make us content? We soon came up with a list:

- Whether we stop at a motel with a pool or use our pop-up camper.
- Whether we get to go to Yellowstone or need to stay home for a year.
- Whether I have designer jeans or a cousin's hand-me-downs.
- Whether Mom's cupboards are full or it's the day before payday.

Then Grace said,"How come there isn't a Scripture chorus for this well-known verse? There's music for Matthew 6:33" (Seek Ye First) "and Philippians 4:4" (Rejoice in the Lord Always) "and so many others—why not this one?" We began trying to make up a tune.

Here's what we created, as transcribed by Nathan over the *next* fifty miles.

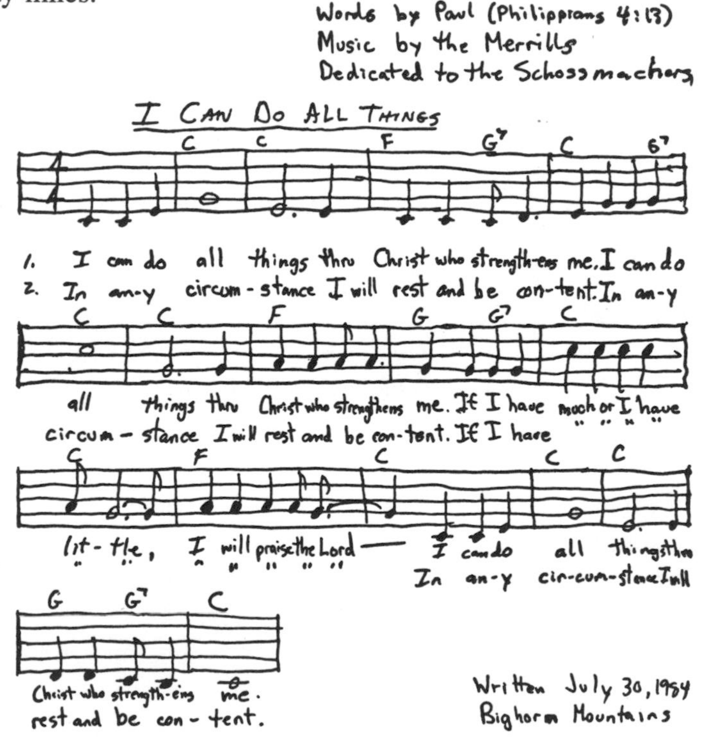

It's certainly not a composition worthy of Mozart, but it meant a great deal to our family and has continued to be sung around our house. Soon after returning home, we recorded it on a cassette to send to some friends who were just beginning missionary itineration. It was one of those spontaneous times that turned out to be very special.

Anyone can try writing a Scripture song. Just choose a verse and start humming. Whether or not it makes you famous is beside the point. You are singing a new song to the Lord.

Once you stop for the night, you can pick up the spiritual thread again. Camping families have special opportunities to sit around a fire and sing, tell Bible stories, share personal dreams and hopes, and pray together. Kids are in a specially receptive mood while staring at the flames.

Some Christian camps provide actual family camp weeks, with some programming but lots of free times, too. They're worth researching.

Church attendance is another valid vacation event. In fact, you can use the opportunity to expose your children to a church of a different size or style than your own. Many state and national parks provide nondenominational Sunday morning worship in outdoor amphitheaters, which is a special experience. Otherwise, head into town and find a congregation to visit.

Rolling across Nebraska, Nathan said, "Sometime I want to see what a Catholic Mass is like." Our family, being Protestant, had never had that experience, but many of his classmates are Catholic. We thought about it and decided if he was curious about Mass, he might as well find out now—with us alongside. So the last Sunday of the trip, we stopped at a Catholic church in Tomah, Wisconsin.

On the way to the car afterward, nine-year-old Rhonda quietly announced, "I have a *million* questions." We spent that lunch hour talking about what we'd seen and heard, explaining symbols, sorting out impressions. It was a valuable day.

Special Times Nearby

If you can't swing a cross-country trip, you can have almost as much fun spending a night at a nearby motel or hotel with a pool. Check in at the earliest allowed time and concentrate on the kids for the next twenty-four hours. If you need to economize, bring along your own food for lunch, snacks, and breakfast, going out to a restaurant only for the evening meal.

Limit TV watching to just one quality program in the evening (if you can find it), and spend the rest of the time with favorite table games or storytelling. Everyone crawl into bed, turn out the lights, and continue talking (something that normally isn't allowed). Tell jokes, early memories, or dreams of the future.

By the time you check out the next day, you won't have spent very much money, and you'll feel like you've been away forever. You'll probably decide to do the same thing again in the middle of winter, which works just as well.

One other special event that's not hard to do at all: Invite each child to breakfast alone with Dad or Mom sometime during the summer. Go ahead and put it on the calendar weeks in advance, to build the anticipation. You'll find yourself in the presence of a very flattered child who is likely to share deepest feelings and thoughts with you. What more could a parent ask?

Both of us encourage you to *choose* to accept the opportunity of a rich, God-centered summer with your children.

How Dad and Mom Found Each Other: Parents' Anniversary

Chances are, you've always thought of your wedding anniversary in terms of adults only. It's a night to hire a baby-sitter and go out on the town.

Nothing wrong with that! But at the same time, kids are curious about your beginnings as a couple. And they need positive examples of how a life partner is discovered. What happened to the two of you is probably a lot more exemplary than what they see on TV or in movies these days.

So on the family night closest to your anniversary, do a candlelight dinner with the children. As the meal progresses, tell all the juicy circumstances of how you met, what you thought of each other at first, the ups and downs of dating, what you thought of your potential in-laws, and how you eventually knew (if you were paying attention to God in those days) that this person was God's choice for you. If you weren't Christians at the time, confess that, and show any ways God seemed to work in spite of you.

Let your children see the twinkle in your eyes as you recount those special months and years. Describe your engagement. Get out wedding photos or slides, perhaps the ringbearer's pillow or a wedding veil; let your daughter try it on.

You might mention that God does call some people to be single, and that's all right. It doesn't mean they're strange. The apostle Paul, in fact, said it was a good idea if you're going to be absorbed, as he was, in the Lord's work (see 1 Cor. 7:29-35).

On the other hand, your children are likely to marry. Talk about the fact that "*right now* somewhere in the world is probably a boy, a girl, about your age whom the Lord has in mind to be your husband, your wife! And if you stay close to Jesus and keep checking his opinion as you get older, he'll guide you to that special person just as he did the two of us. He'll help you make the very best decision."

Take time to pray for these unknown future spouses, for their education, their protection, their walk with Christ, their maturity. In this way you build a view of the future—and an alternative to Hollywood's unrealistic messages about love and marriage.

Relevant Scriptures: Psalm 37:4; Proverbs 3:5-6.

Part Three

Other Times Together

What Shall We Pray About?

How does a child (or grown-up) remember what to pray for? Every parent has listened to bedtime prayers that sounded verbatim to last week's or last year's. This, by the way, is not just a problem for children; adult prayers are sometimes a yawn, too.

Here's a solution: During a Home Together Night, consign each prayer need to a separate three-by-five card. Help each other think of all the legitimate requests you can. Finally, put each person's stack of cards into a plastic holder.

Then each night at bedtime, pull out the deck and pray together for the next one or two cards in line. That way, you don't have to go through everything every night, but neither do you forget certain needs for months on end. Each night is different, and each night is specific.

When a prayer is answered, write what happened on the card and then celebrate throwing it into the wastebasket (or keep it in a separate place for remembering).

One necessity: Update the cards periodically, again on a family night. Spend time brainstorming what new parts of your lives need God's attention. . . new friends who have needs. . . upcoming challenges.

Make sure the cards include not only Grandma's high blood pressure and the school friend's dad who isn't a Christian, but also things like "that I'll be a real Christian at school."

This method covers the petition and intercession aspects of prayer. But there's also praise, thanksgiving, and confession. To remember these, add a special card to the deck—perhaps in bright orange or lavender—that is to be used *every* time. The card reads:

"I appreciate you, Lord, because you're. . ."

"Thank you for. . ."

"I'm sorry for the way I. . . . Please forgive me."

When praying together as a whole family, it's good to name the prayer topics before you start—and sometimes even to assign them to individuals. "Kim, how about if you pray for your friend at school whose parents are breaking up. I'll take the decision about whether we should trade cars, and Mike, you pray for our pastors and elders at church, that they'll be good leaders." This gives everyone a track to run on.

At other times, however, experiment with conversational prayer. Start out with brief sentences of thankfulness. Then say, "Let's now tell the Lord how we feel about vacation this coming summer." Each person may voice what's on his or her mind. There's no rule about speaking only once. If you think of something else you wanted to say, go ahead.

Then move to another subject.

This may be stop-start the first few times, but eventually it will begin to flow. Children are not great speechmakers anyway, and as soon as they realize it's all right to talk in an ordinary manner with God, they'll participate with ease.

Kids and the Urge to Talk Back

One Scripture passage our family has never had trouble understanding is James 3:6-9—the dangers of the tongue. When the apostle writes, "The tongue also is a fire, a world of evil . . . a restless evil, full of deadly poison," we know exactly what he's talking about.

One week when the younger members of the tribe seemed especially mouthy (wonder where they learned it?), Father and Mother decided it was time for some friendly instruction. (We did not reprimand the kids during the presentation, however, or harangue them about past offenses. Home Together Night is always positive.)

We sat in a semicircle around a chalkboard and made Nathan the scribe. He wrote as we called out as many ways to use our mouths as we could think of: whistling, crying, eating, talking, whispering, saying bad words, laughing, pouting, whining, praying, arguing, being sassy, kissing . . .

Then we looked up James 1:19 and talked about what it means to be "quick to listen, slow to speak and slow to become angry." We passed the eraser around so each person could rub out an inappropriate action on our list, something that displeases Jesus. We prayed for control in this area of our lives and then sang the familiar children's song "Oh, Be Careful, Little Mouths, What You Say."

After a teaching this serious, we closed off the evening with a few rousing rounds of a popular game at the time, "Mr. Mouth." Kids and adults alike had fun flipping plastic chips into a battery-powered creature that opens and closes its mouth as it rotates.

Throughout the following week, we memorized James 1:19. This verse is especially good and clear for children. It's also realistic, in that it doesn't tell us *never* to become angry. It merely says to heat up slowly! Other succinct Scriptures on the same theme: Psalm 141:3; Proverbs 15:23; 17:27; and 25:11.

On another August night, just before school started and our children plunged into the world of boasting and bumping, slang and slurs, we returned to the theme of mouth control. Sitting with Bibles in the backyard, we took a tour of Proverbs, mainly 12:13-19, which includes such easy-to-understand lines as "An evil man is trapped by his sinful talk, but a righteous man escapes trouble. . . . A fool shows his annoyance at once, but a prudent man overlooks an insult. . . . Reckless words pierce like a sword, but the tongue of the wise brings healing." Applying these verses to the school scene wasn't hard!

Other stops on our tour: Proverbs 13:10; 15:1, 23; 16:24; 17:1; and even 21:9 (with Grace's permission).

We then went around the circle completing these sentences:

"I like to talk about __________."

"I get upset when I hear __________."

Since all of our children would be heading to new schools the next week (the girls were starting a year of preschool, and due to a boundary change, third-grade Nathan was switching schools), we got in the car and went on a second tour. We drove to both new playgrounds and let them play on the equipment. Our purpose was twofold: to gain familiarity with the new surroundings, and also to start imagining what it would be like to control their tongues in these settings.

Three years later, would you believe the subject still needed attention? By this time, Rhonda and Tricia were at the stage of loving puppet play. In fact, we had cut a huge carton (which had housed our new refrigerator) into a puppet theater, spray-painting it a garish red. (Impromptu puppet shows can work almost as well, however, simply by kneeling behind a table or couch.)

So we said, "The two of you be the performers tonight, and the three of us will be the audience. Here are four starter ideas, all of which are about the theme of 'How to Vent Acceptably.' In each of these, somebody will really want to blow off steam.

"You take the play up to the point of 'explosion'—then stop. We, the audience, will then suggest *two* different ways to finish the story." (That way, everyone got a piece of the action.)

The starter ideas:

- Early evening at home: Dad forgets, for the second day, to bring scrap paper from the office (the kids' main source for drawing and coloring).
- The supper table: two kids disagree on whether the beans come from our garden or out of a can.
- On the swing set: two people want the trapeze at the same time.
- A gorgeous Saturday morning: a friend wants to play, but a bedroom hasn't been cleaned yet.

(As you have probably guessed, none of the above were fiction. All came from recent history at the Merrill house.)

The puppet disputes, of course, were loud and occasionally violent. Thinking of peaceful solutions (such as one kid enjoying the trapeze while the other counts to one hundred, then switching) took some effort, but it wasn't impossible. Dad's closing point was that Philippians 2:14 ("Do everything without complaining or arguing") isn't just a line thought up by some weary parent; it really is God's Word, and that means we must obey it—all of us. God knew what he was talking about, and he wouldn't have given us this commandment if we couldn't do it.

The Family That Cares: Reaching Out to Others

Who taught you to reach out to others? Who taught you to extend yourself to the sick, the aged, the needy? Who broke you out of your toddler mindset ("Me first! Mine!") and showed you what it meant to love people in Christ's stead?

This extension doesn't happen naturally, you know. Self-centeredness will reign unchecked in any human being, regardless of age, unless *someone* says, "Look up. See the needs around you. Feel the pain. Now reach out. . .touch. . .love."

Grace remembers a line from a sermon years ago that asked poignantly, "Are the arrows of your life pointed out or in?" The pastor spoke of arrows not as weapons but rather as extensions of concern and attention. So much of our personal difficulty, he went on to explain, comes from focusing on ourselves, *our* rights, *our* hurts. Many a marriage, and some churches as well, has been split because of this.

But if the arrows travel outward, across the gaps that isolate us all, we build a loving community.

Once again, parents are the first-line models for children.

There is no lack of opportunity. You can prepare a meal *as a family* (not just Mom) and take it together to a home where there is sickness or a new baby. Or you can simply make cookies and go for a time of snacks and singing. Once we did this for a man whose leg had been severely shattered in an industrial accident; he hadn't been able to come to church for months. We took along a guitar and simply sang together.

We debated another time about whether to take the children to the home of a forty-year-old man, the father of one of Nathan's friends, in the advanced stages of cancer. We finally decided there was no reason to leave them home. We told them in advance that since Mr. Johnson was weak, we could not stay long. But they should treat him normally, talk freely, not be afraid to touch him, and give him smiles and encouragement.

It was a moving experience to sing and recite Scripture that evening, and when we prayed together, there were tears. But there was also profuse appreciation from the Johnsons for our coming. We had brought a little piece of ''church'' to the house of the dying. One month later to the day, he entered heaven.

Hospitals often have rules about the minimum age of visitors, but we've learned it often pays to ask for an exception. If you call ahead and say, ''Our children have made a special poster (or banner) for so-and-so, and we'd like to stop very briefly Tuesday evening to deliver it,'' it takes a pretty tough nurse to say no. We've succeeded in taking our children not only into pediatrics but also the adult wards as well.

If the regulations cannot be bent, however, you can still make the poster, go as a family to the lounge, and wait there while one parent delivers your handiwork to the patient.

One Scripture we've used on several posters is Exodus 14:14—"The Lord will fight for you; you need only to be still." When the children's Grandpa Danielson was intensely ill with pneumonia several years ago, we made a felt banner showing a sunrise and cut out the letters for a phrase from Psalm 57:8 (TLB)—"Greet the dawn with song!" It was placed directly at the foot of his bed to speak its message each morning as he opened his eyes.

One Home Together Night we put together a box of fun things for an eleven-year-old girl we had only heard about who was in a Wisconsin hospital for a kidney transplant. Her mother had recently died, and a family in our church was concerned about her. That, to us, was reason enough to reach out with an expression of Jesus' love.

Is there a nursing home near your house? You don't have to get a large group together for visiting or putting on a simple program;

a family is fine. The elderly *adore* children. Nathan played his very first public trombone solo in such a place and was, of course, warmly received and congratulated. That made the first solo in church not so scary.

Others in need of our arrows of contact are neither sick nor old but just lonely. When one of our pastors was in the Orient for a missionary trip, we took his wife and children out for pizza. We brought along an aerogramme, drew lines to create nine boxes, and each wrote a note to send to the absent father. Then we smeared red pizza sauce along the edges to make him homesick! So simple to do—but so special to receive, as he reported when he got back.

Food naturally bespeaks friendship. Kids will enjoy making chocolate chip cookies with you on a family night, arranging them on several paper plates, covering them with plastic wrap, and attaching tags that say only, "Happy Ordinary Day!" No name—just the greeting.

Then sneak around to deliver them to neighbors' porches, or to those of lonely people you know. Ring the doorbell and run!

We have no idea how far-reaching will be the effect of this kind of modeling once our children become adults. We must simply obey the injunction of Galatians 6:9-10 (good memory verses, by the way)—"Let us not become weary in doing good, for at the proper time we will reap a harvest if we do not give up. Therefore, as we have opportunity, let us do good to all people, especially to those who belong to the family of believers."

From Adam to Zerubbabel: A Game for the Car

Here's an oldie-but-goodie Bible game to play in the car. You probably heard of it long ago and have since forgotten it. It's worth resurrecting because it's fun, it teaches Bible knowledge, and it requires no props.

One family member begins, "I'm thinking of a Bible person whose name begins with M" (or whatever).

Going clockwise around the car, the others guess who. But *not* by name (that's too easy). By a description of some kind—*which the original person must identify.*

"Was it the mother of Jesus?"

"No, it was not Mary."

"Was it the tax collector?"

"No, it was not Matthew."

"Was it the baby who floated in a basket in the river?"

"Yes, it was Moses!"

The person who finally elicits a yes answer gets to give the next alphabet clue. (Warning: the J's are the worst! The possibilities go on forever, from Japheth to Jacob to Joseph [O.T.] to Joshua to Jehoshaphat to Jeremiah to Joseph [N.T.] to John the Baptist to Jesus to John the disciple to two or three different Jameses to Judas to. . .)

If one player wins too many consecutive yeses, he or she can be asked to donate a turn to someone else.

The genius of this simple game is that everyone has to contribute Bible knowledge.

Younger players sometimes need help thinking of descriptions. They can whisper to Mom or Dad, "What did Samson do?" "He was the strongest man in the Bible." Then they can proceed to ask their question. Young players likewise may get stumped from time to time and need to be bailed out.

It's probably best not to enact penalties, such as loss of turn, for these things. Keep the atmosphere fun; that's when the most learning takes place.

Lest We Forget: When Grandparents Come to Visit

Sometimes the most important stories never get told.

In an earlier, pre-television age, youngsters sat on front porches swatting mosquitoes and listening to their elders recount the family heritage. Now, between soccer practice and sitcoms, the time for oral history has largely been lost.

But not necessarily. When grandparents come to visit on family night, the stage is set for stoking the memories and igniting the imaginations of children. Since they don't know what stories to ask for, and the visitors don't know whether we really want to hear, it is up to us—the middle generation—to say, "Grandpa, tell about the time you . . ."

One Home Together Night, our sole teaching activity was listening to Grandpa Merrill recount the night his first-grade son Dean asked at bedtime, "How do you become a Christian?" He described the small house in Texas where the family lived, and the way Dean procrastinated until prayers had already been said and he was tucked into bed before bringing up this greatest of all subjects. Grandpa told how he explained, in simple language, that anyone who confessed his sins and asked Christ to forgive him would be accepted into God's family forevermore. Then came the getting out of bed again, the kneeling and praying, and the rejoicing . . .

Dean could have told the story himself. But it meant more coming from the family patriarch.

On another evening, Grandpa Danielson told his boyhood escapade of stealing apples from a neighbor's farm. Using real apples for props, he tucked them into his shirt that night as he had nearly seventy years previous, trying to avoid detection. His grandchildren's eyes grew wide. Grandpa, a *pastor* all his life, had once *stolen?*

His lumpy midsection had not escaped his mother's discerning eye. Soon he was back on the road to confess his crime to the neighbors. They accepted his apology and said that in the future, *if he asked*, he could have an apple anytime.

Following the story came the evening's closing treat for everyone: apples, of course.

Grandparents have much to share that is of infinite value. They won't be available forever. Will they get the chance?

If You Controlled the Checkbook: Teaching About Finances

Whenever, financially speaking, "your ship comes in"—your income tax refund arrives, or your Christmas bonus is paid, or an inheritance comes through—you can use the occasion to help your children learn about spending.

Start out by reading together Luke 12:13-15. Retell the story in your own words: "Here are two brothers with a bundle of money for once, and they're fighting about it. It's gotten to be a huge argument. What does Jesus say? How does he solve the problem?

"What does the last half of verse 15 mean?"

Then go on to read verses 16-21, the story of the rich fool. Again, dramatize the events and ask, "Why do you think God called him a fool? That's pretty strong language!"

Then say, "Let's see if we handle our money better than these people did. If *you* were making the decisions instead of Mom and Dad, what would you do?"

When we did this in our family, we didn't particularly want the kids knowing the exact dollar amount we had received. So Dean converted everything to points and listed them on a chalkboard. He said, "Mom and I have already given the Lord his 10 percent, and now we have 48 points left. The possibilities are:

The used sewing machine Mom would like	1
New living room furniture	11
A better trombone for Nathan	6
A deck for the backyard	3
A home computer	22
A used organ	10
Save the money for kids' college	0-48

This gave them a sense of proportion among the items; the only thing they didn't know (and didn't need to know) was the dollar equivalent of a point. Obviously, there weren't enough points for everything on this list (which is how it always is in life, right?). How would they choose?

Each child was given a piece of scratch paper to make his or her list. Then each read the results and defended them. The idea of saving for college was less popular with some than with others.

We parents learned from this what their most fervent wishes were. We concluded by saying that although Mom and Dad would have to make the final choices, we were glad for their input and would take it into consideration. They had thought seriously about the uses of money—and they'd be in our shoes soon enough.

What Does "Hallowed" Mean? The Lord's Prayer for Kids

It's easy to assume our children understand things they don't—especially classic texts of Scripture. The Lord's Prayer, for example, belongs in every child's brain. But do those majestic words mean very much to a second-grader?

We decided to find out one night by attempting the "Merrill paraphrase." We drew a line down the middle of a piece of bright construction paper, wrote the venerable King James version on the left side (Matt. 6:9-13), and then had the kids take turns playing secretary on the right side. We jointly began recasting the prayer, phrase by phrase. As they tried to create various wordings, all sorts of uncertainties came to light.

We did a lot of clarifying, and the final version (which stayed on the refrigerator for weeks) turned out as follows:

> Dear heavenly daddy, who lives in heaven,
> *[a little redundancy there, but. . .]*
> Your name is very special.
> I want to obey you here on earth,
> just like the angels do in heaven.
> Thank you for all our food each day.
> Forgive me my sins, and I want to forgive people
> who do wrong to me.
> When I think about doing something wrong,
> help me to do right instead.
> For you are the most powerful king
> there ever will be. Amen.

Whether all the fine points of theology were represented or not, this made the Lord's Prayer manageable to three children. It deepened their understanding, which was our goal.

This approach will work with any number of important biblical passages. It amounts to a type of Bible study—but in a fresh way that can revitalize an excessively familiar part of God's Word.

The Forgotten Part of Prayer: Confession

What's the easiest thing to say when talking to God?

For children and adults alike, the answer is probably thanksgiving. "Thank you, Lord, for my food/bed/house/dog/bike/mom and dad/you-name-it" flows naturally from young pray–ers.

What else comes easily? Intercession. "Please help Grandma feel better." Adoration ("I love you, Lord") takes a bit more training. But the real stickler is confession.

Once you've messed up in the course of a day (yelled at your sister, raided the cookie jar, blamed Kevin for the flowers you smashed with a basketball)—why bring up the subject *again?*

The same holds for parents who cheat on their diets, overbook their schedules at the family's expense, or fail to muster the willpower to turn off the TV when it needs it.

One Home Together Night we talked about this, noting that our bedtime prayers frequently omitted confession. We noted that Jesus gave us a clear example, however, in his model prayer: "Forgive us our trespasses" (that last word took a bit of explaining).

We talked about *why* we should go through the discomfort of confessing: to clear the air with God, to let him know we understand we did wrong, to lay a foundation for doing differently next time.

Finally, we said, "All right, let's not just talk about it. Let's each go to a separate room, kneel down, and spend a few minutes asking God's forgiveness. You don't have to tell the rest of us what you confess. When you're done, come back to the living room."

The kids seemed intent as they walked away to do private business with their heavenly Father. It was a genuine exercise for them. Dad and Mom needed it, too.

The Secret of Scripture Memory

In this age of electronic data retrieval, Scripture memorization has fallen on hard times. The idea of storing any text *in your head* seems old-fashioned (plus a lot of work).

At our house, we still take Psalm 119:11 at face value when it says hiding God's Word in the heart is a strategic hedge against sin. It is one of the answers to the preceding question (verse 9a), "How can a young man keep his way pure?"

But Christian parents and teachers who want children to memorize God's Word have to face a simple fact of life: *Memorization without review is nothing.* Zero. A waste of time.

Shouldn't that be obvious? Stop a minute and try to recall your telephone number two or three towns ago. You used to know it perfectly. Why can't you come up with it now?

Because you haven't had any need to review.

The average grade-schooler's mind can stash away prodigious amounts of Scripture (or song lyrics, or baseball batting averages, or baton troupe routines). The young brain is a vast field of invisible grooves in a small space, just waiting for input. It's a matter of easy-in but also easy-out. Hence, the need for a retention system.

We've inherited our system from Dean's childhood. Somewhere around age four, his parents began writing on three by five cards the verses he memorized in Sunday school as well as at their initiative. The verse was recorded on one side, the reference on the other, and the cards were kept in a recipe box. As soon as he learned to write, he was allowed to do his own copying from the Bible. (These specimens of his earliest handwriting are now priceless.)

New verses were added at an average of one a week for the next ten or twelve years, so that his collection eventually topped out at around six hundred verses. And one or more times a week, his mother would sit down with him to listen to recitation, one card after another. A stiff cardboard marker moved through the deck, from Genesis 1:1 to Revelation 20:15, and then back to the front again.

The result? Today, more than thirty years later, the vast majority of those Scriptures have "stuck."

Each of our three children now has a box of his or her own that is gradually filling up. New cards sit on the kitchen table alongside the salt and pepper for mealtime study between bites. Within a few days, they're ready to be added to the boxes.

Sometimes if all three children are working on the same text, we'll do a round robin exercise in which each person says just two words of the verse ("The Lord—was with—Samuel as—he grew—up, and—he let—none of—his words—fall to—the ground" 1 Sam. 3:19). Starting at a different point each round, the verse is mastered in three or four go-arounds. As mentioned above, we incorporate verses assigned in Sunday school or midweek clubs at church; we also supplement others of our own choosing.

One goal, just for the novelty of it, is to memorize at least one useful verse from each of the Bible's sixty-six books. (In some cases, that takes some searching!) Another project (mentioned in the chapter "Summer: Ordeal or Opportunity?") is to conquer an entire chapter of the Bible.

Reciting the bank of verses is a standard part of family life, usually after supper a couple of nights a week (*not* Home Together Night, since this is a one-to-one activity). We have learned the hard way to stick with it, despite a busy life-style. The longer the gaps between review, the rustier the kids' memories become, and the more the whole process becomes drudgery. On the other hand, the more frequently we review, the easier the phrases come, and the more fun for everyone. It's a case of use it or lose it.

And occasionally, the kids turn the tables and haul out Dad's box from childhood. They want to see if the old man still knows his Scripture.

The great truths of God's Word do no good lying ink-bound in a closed book. If we mean for the next generation to *live* godly lives, we must take the time to implant those parameters in their very beings. Review systems such as the above may vary from home to home, but the goal must never be forgotten.

All the Home's a Stage: Dramatizing Bible Stories

Playacting a Bible story is standard teaching procedure with grade-school kids—but there are at least four reasons why it is *especially* effective in a family setting.

1. The limited size of the "cast" (mom, dad, and kids) means everybody gets a "good" part. Most stories center on no more than half a dozen characters. So what happens in a classroom of twenty-five? A lot of kids have to be "part of the crowd" or else just watch. Not so at home. Everybody gets a chance to star.
2. Many stories take place in two or more scenes. Again, a classroom is no match for a home, which has separate rooms. The action can move from kitchen to family room to bedroom, however the story line unfolds.
3. Parents and kids are drawn closer by joining in a common production. The gap is especially narrowed when Dad assumes a subservient role while Christy gets to be Jesus, or King David, or whomever.
4. Props are instantly available. Overcoats, bathrobes, baseball bats for clubs or swords, tableware, paper crowns, cooking pots turned upside-down for soldiers' helmets. . .they're all at hand to enliven the visual effect.

Here are some examples of Bible stories our family dramatized:

How God Helps in Desperate Situations (Acts 12)

We used the story of Peter's great deliverance from prison the night we were taking care of two guests: first-grader Jeff and his four-year-old sister Kelly. We awarded Jeff the plum role (Peter) and Kelly became Rhoda, the overjoyed servant at the house of Mary (Grace). Two of our children were the arresting soldiers, while the other played the angel, and Dad was the wicked King

Herod.

The kitchen became the king's court; the soldiers nabbed Peter somewhere beyond the breakfast table and hauled him to a darkened family room. Once asleep, the angel entered, flipped a switch, ushered the groggy apostle out, and slipped away. Peter then approached the dining room, where Mary and Rhoda were engaged in a fervent prayer meeting. His loud knock brought all manner of exclamations and joyous embraces.

Such theater is always worth a repeat performance, of course. The first time through is really a rehearsal to get the lines and movements down; the second time, the kids really get into their roles and begin improvising. Two times naturally make the point of the play clearer: God sometimes waits quite a while, but he does come through when his people are in trouble.

The play's impact was revealed the next day when Jeff and Kelly's parents returned to pick them up. One of the first things Jeff wanted to announce was "Dad, I got to be Peter!"

Standing Up to Pressure (Daniel 3)

Every Christian parent knows that running with the herd comes natural to children (and most adults); we have to *work* for enough self-confidence to take a minority position. Yet God's way is frequently in the minority. Perhaps the most dramatic example in Scripture is Shadrach, Meshach, and Abednego vs. the king and his fiery furnace. It has all the tension and excitement of a schoolyard face-off.

We acted this a number of years ago on a Home Together Night, and we've forgotten who played which roles. (Tall Dad was probably the ninety-foot image of gold!) Anyway, the play proceeded with most actors bowing down as ordered, one or two refusing, and Nebuchadnezzar summoning the offenders to the kitchen, where all four burners on the range were flaming brightly. (We may have fired up the oven in advance, too.) There, with the heat turning faces crimson, the children uttered those lines of conviction: "If we are thrown into the blazing furnace, the God we serve is able to save us from it. . . . But even if he does not, we want you to know, O king, that we will not serve your gods. . . ."

Nobody was actually hoisted up onto the range, of course, but with a bit of pretending, the king soon saw the fourth man in the flames and expressed his shock. He then ended the play with his about-face decree that the Lord God should be respected.

What's the purpose of this? To plant in young minds a critical idea: *I can stand up for what's right. I don't have to go along with what everybody else is doing. If I go God's way, he'll defend me.*

Listening the First Time (Numbers 22)

The Bible's one instance of a talking donkey is a natural favorite of kids. Balaam, the uncertain prophet, learns the hard way to pay attention to God's instructions no matter what the king's messengers say or do.

Again, this story needs two stages: the court of King Balak and the prophet's home, with a "road" in between. The actors include the prophet, the king, at least one messenger, an angel with fearsome sword, and the donkey. This last part is, of course, reserved for Dad, on whose back Balaam gleefully gets to ride. (Is anything more delightful for a grade-school kid?)

If your children haven't heard the story in a while, you may need to read it first from a modern translation. A humorous talking-monologue version is also available in Don Francisco's "Balaam" on his *Got to Tell Somebody* cassette (NewPax). Then, curtain's up!

Riding the Wind: Lessons for Windy Days

It was a breezy spring evening. What better thing to do this family night than fly kites in the park?

But we also wanted the children to begin memorizing a special passage to recite at their grandparents' golden anniversary celebration in June. We had selected the elegant words of Psalm 37:23-25 (KJV): "The steps of a good man are ordered by the LORD: and he delighteth in his way. Though he fall, he shall not be utterly cast down: for the LORD upholdeth him with his hand. I have been young, and now am old; yet have I not seen the righteous forsaken, nor his seed begging bread."

Grace parceled out verses, one to each child, and got them copying their portions onto three-by-five cards for their memory boxes (see "The Secret of Scripture Memory" for a fuller explanation of this approach). She didn't drill them long; one tactic we've learned is that several quick hits over several days accomplish more than one marathon session of trying to get the Scripture word-perfect the first time.

Meanwhile, Dean was unwinding a new ball of kite string throughout the other rooms of the house, in and out of bedrooms, down to the basement, and back up—and hiding a kite at the far end. Actually, the trail was simpler than it looked; it had few cross-overs (so as to minimize tangles!). But to the eyes of young children, it looked like a full-scale maze.

"Now we'll see how well you can 'order' *your steps*," he announced. "In a way, this will be like Grandpa and Grandma following God's direction back and forth, up and down all through their lives and coming to a good end. You wind up the string as best you can, and you'll discover something neat at the end."

Soon we were on our way to the park to fly the new toy. And

the kids had a mental picture to associate with their new verses.

A different kind of wind propelled us to another application on a winter Home Together Night. An Illinois blizzard was howling outside, with wind gusts so strong the weather stripping around our front door would vibrate every so often with an eerie moan.

We scrapped whatever teaching we had planned for that night and huddled instead inside a huge quilt on the floor. We hugged each other and listened to the raging wind for a full minute or two before Dean said, "This is what it sounded like the night Jesus and his disciples got caught in the storm on Galilee. We don't even want to be outdoors tonight. Can you imagine being outdoors in a boat on a lake!"

He went on to recount the story of Jesus' calming the wind and waves (Mark 4:35-41). The children knew the story from earlier classes, of course, but on this night, with nature's abundant sound effects, it carried a special power. A Christ who could stop a storm like *this* blizzard must be mighty indeed!

Sibling Rivalry Is Nothing New

If you have two or more children, and if they ever fight (does the bear live in the woods?), you may be relieved to know the Bible is *full* of cases of sibling rivalry.

And since the problem is hardly solved by parental nagging, you may be looking for more positive ways to help small brothers and sisters get along—or at least coexist peacefully.

How about a family night tour of some of the following?

- *Cain and Abel* (Gen. 4:2-16), who show what happens when jealousy gets out of hand.
- *Isaac and Ishmael* (Gen. 21:8-20), where ridicule ended up splitting the family.
- *Esau and Jacob* (Gen. 25:27-34 and chap. 27)—two brothers very *dis*similar, and one of them very deceptive. But see also Genesis 33 for the belated truce.
- *Joseph and his brothers* (Gen. 37 and 42-45), who could not handle a father's well-meaning favoritism.
- *Miriam, Aaron, and Moses* (Num. 12), another jealousy situation.
- *David and his older brothers*, who argue before the duel with Goliath (1 Sam. 17:17-32).
- *Amnon and Tamar* (2 Sam. 13)—skip this one unless you're willing to talk about incest!
- *Adonijah and Solomon* battling for their father's throne (1 Kings 1; also 2:13-25).
- *James and John*, ambitious and hot-headed (Luke 9:49-56; Mark 10:35-45).
- *Martha, Mary, and Lazarus*, arguing over household chores (Luke 10:38-42) but also loving each other intensely (John 11).

There's enough here for a series of family circle times if you take them a few at a time. If your children are young, you may want to summarize some of the longer passages or read from a children's Bible storybook. Older children can take it straight from the Scripture.

Or you can assign each family member a *different* set of siblings to read about individually and then report to the rest. Ground to be covered:

- What were these brothers/sisters like?
- How did they get along—or not?
- What consequences did they have to pay because of not getting along?
- What would you have said if you could have talked to them? What could they have done better?
- Did God try to influence them at all or just let them go on fighting?
- What's one lesson for our family from this story?

Moving Day

Close friends of ours were moving—and were less than thrilled about it. The demands of career had been weighed and finally agreed to, but butterflies still lingered.

The moving van had already left, and they joined us for supper that Home Together Night, a last meal before we would take them to the train. Their two daughters sat quietly, absorbing as much of the familiar as they could before all would turn strange and different.

Amid the hamburgers, applesauce, and iced tea, Dean proposed an offbeat idea: "Let's think through the Bible and name people who *moved*."

Well, let's see: there was Abram and Sarai and all their stuff—they moved several times. Jacob and his clan, down to Egypt. The Israelites, back to the Promised Land. David spent several years running from Saul. Daniel and his friends got moved to Babylon, like it or not. And then, of course, Mary and Joseph. . . It soon turned into a game.

"So you guys aren't the only ones ever to do this, are you? Other people have moved, and survived. In fact, God even told some of them to move, and he took care of the whole process." The air in the room seemed to lighten.

If we'd had more time, we would have read some of God's words to movers (Gen. 12:1-3; Deut. 1:6-8; Matt. 2:13-15, 19-23). But it was time to head for the depot.

It is important to draw parallels between our stresses and those of God's people in the past—whenever valid parallels exist—to learn from them. That's why God invested so much of his Book in people stories. "These things happened to them as examples," says 1 Corinthians 10:11. The same paragraph goes on to state, ". . .God is faithful; he will not let you be tempted beyond what you can bear. But when you are tempted [to throw up your hands and scream in the middle of packing, and so forth], he will also provide a way out so that you can stand up under it'' (v. 13).

Moving is a great trauma for many children, and it is a comfort to know that even this is not beyond the control of God.

Who's in Charge of the Family?

Young couples sometimes fantasize about egalitarian home life, where sweet reason prevails and all decisions are reached by consensus. Then children arrive!

It doesn't take long to discover that kids are occasionally lacking in calm objectivity (ditto for parents) and, therefore, not all decisions will be greeted with smiles and applause. We finally came to the time when we decided there was too much ambivalence among the troops about where the buck stopped. Accordingly, on Home Together Night we passed out various colors of construction paper to each family member and said, "Draw and cut out a full-length picture of yourself." That was fun enough.

Then we produced string, a punch, and a coat hanger. "Now we're going to put our cut-outs together into a mobile," we announced.

"Who goes on top? Who's in charge of the whole family?" Answer: God. We rummaged for a piece of gold wrapping paper, cut it into an oval, cut out construction paper letters G-O-D, pasted them on, and pasted the oval to the coat hanger.

Next we strung the figure of Dad under God, followed by Mom. This reflected our understanding of Scripture's teaching about family structure and responsibility. (We realize some couples would read the same Scripture and choose to place themselves parallel.) Next came a horizontal straw suspended from both Dad and Mom like a trapeze, from which hung the three figures of the kids. If we'd had our dog Frisky at the time, she would have come last.

We hung the completed mobile from the curtain rod beside the kitchen table, admired each other's self-portraits, but also studied the relationships illustrated.

Do kids tell parents what to do? No.

Do parents tell God what to do? No.

Do kids tell each other what to do? No.

Do parents tell kids what to do? Yes.

Does God tell parents what to do? Yes.

How does God tell kids what to do? Mainly through parents.

What will happen when you finish school and move out on your own? You'll move up and into the middle, so a string will run directly from God to you. The middle rank will be removed.

And then what will happen if you marry and have children? You'll have a straw of your own, with others for whom you'll be responsible.

"We want you to know," we said, "that it's an awesome thing for us to be directed by God for your lives. We don't take it lightly. We really aren't smart enough to raise you alone. We need his direction, and we try to pass it on to you as best we can.

"We also look forward to the day when you take your place in the same level as we are now."

In previous generations, this kind of activity probably wouldn't have been needed. As Haim Ginott says in one of his books, "Whatever grandfather did was done with authority; whatever we do is done with hesitation. Even when in error, grandfather acted with certainty. Even when in the right, we act with doubt."

Sometimes we are too flexible and accommodating for our own good. While we should not be tyrants, neither should we be jellyfish. A clear statement of how the household runs—along with a glimpse of the future—is sometimes helpful.

Instruments of Praise

It was one of those Tuesdays when an outside scheduler (in this case, Nathan's school) had unknowingly infringed on Home Together Night. The year-end band concert was set for 7:30 P.M.

Rather than bumping Home Together Night to a different night, we decided to incorporate the concert. After a quick meal that included Grandma and Grandpa, we said, "We're going to start thinking early tonight about band instruments—especially the ways we can use them to praise God." We gave each person a long strip of drawing paper and assigned a verse of Psalm 150 to be portrayed in rebus.

Rebus is the technical name for the mixture of printed text and drawings that every kid loves. Example: "Praise the Lord. Praise God in [*picture of church instead of 'his sanctuary'*]. Praise him in [*picture of nighttime stars and moon instead of 'his mighty heavens'*]."

The easiest verses of this particular psalm for kids to illustrate are 3, 4, and 5, which mention the many instruments of praise. Verses 2 and 6 are perhaps better for adult creativity.

Within minutes the six strips were ready to be taped, ladderlike in sequential order, on a wall. Everyone stood back and gazed at the corporate handiwork. Seven-year-olds and seventy-year-olds had worked on a common project and felt proud of the result. Then we jumped into the car and headed for the school concert.

David Hits the Homemade Tube

A perfectly good Sunday school activity can be "stolen" for family use as well: the homemade "television set" with Bible stories inside. All that's needed is a good-sized cardboard box, a knife, scissors, tape, a yardstick, and two items from almost anyone's junk pile—a broomstick and an old window shade.

You and the kids start by cutting a hole the shape of a TV screen in one side of the box. Then you cut silver-dollar-sized holes in the front corners of the box's top and bottom, four holes in all (see sketch). Unroll the window shade on the floor and slit it lengthwise to a width of sixteen inches or whatever the vertical opening is, plus a little more for overlap. Make light pencil marks along the shade to indicate "screenfuls."

Saw the broomstick in half to serve as two spindles around which you'll wind the shade.

We used this one night to capture the story of Jesus feeding the five thousand (John 6:1-15). We read the story from the Bible,

talked about how to break it into sections, and then each child drew and colored one part in sequence. Dialogue was added in speech balloons, cartoon-style.

Scene 1: Jesus and the hungry crowd

Scene 2: Jesus and disciples discussing what to do

Scene 3: The boy shows up with his lunch

Scene 4: Jesus gives thanks

Scene 5: Everybody eats; surplus baskets to one side

Finally the masterpiece was wound around broomstick A, inserted into the left set of holes, stretched out, and taped to broomstick B—and the show was ready for viewing.

Another night, we added the next story, John 6:16-21 (Jesus walking on the water), which lent itself to some dramatic artwork.

Then a couple of years later we dug out the "TV" again. We'd been out of town the previous Sunday, and so we elected to make up the Sunday school lesson our girls had missed. One phone call to the teacher informed us they were in the middle of a unit on the life of David, and the previous Sunday had been 1 Samuel 20—Jonathan supporting his godly friend no matter what.

On our Home Together Night, we each read an assigned paragraph silently, then told the story in our own words. We talked about why Jonathan didn't just stay out of trouble. Apparently he was loyal to David and his God regardless of the cost.

Each person then drew his segment:

Scene 1: David and Jonathan discussing the problem (vv. 1-11)

Scene 2: Jonathan's plan (vv. 12-24)

Scene 3: The banquet table with its empty chair (vv. 25-29)

Scene 4: King Saul's attack (vv. 30-34)

Scene 5: The sad rendezvous in the field (vv. 35-42)

The "TV" with its new insert remained in the family room for a week after that, as kids stopped by to twist the broomsticks and review their creation.

One other trace remains to this day: a red-marker smudge on the 1 Samuel 20 page of Dean's Bible. It is a memento to be treasured.

"I'll Decide for Myself!"

The march toward independence, falteringly begun in early childhood, picks up real steam in grade-school days. Kids realize that—guess what—they'd like to make some of these life-shaping decisions *themselves!* Needless to say, we parents are not always impressed with their store of wisdom and foresight, and we tend to keep calling the shots as long as possible.

That won't work forever, of course.

So why not talk about it? Decision making is beginning to be shared in these years and will be shared more and more as time goes by. Mom and Dad don't make *all* the decisions even now, but they will continue to help make *some* for years yet to come.

Here's one approach: Tape up a large piece of paper on a wall and title it "DECISIONS." You might add a theme from Scripture like Proverbs 15:20, 22—"A wise son brings joy to his father, but a foolish man despises his mother. . . . Plans fail for lack of counsel, but with many advisers they succeed."

Then draw a rectangle, the horizontal dimension of which is a continuum from "Kids decide alone" (far left) to "Kids and parents decide together" (middle) to "Parents decide alone" (far right).

Ask the children for examples of decisions your family deals with, and where on the continuum you should write them down. Here are some examples from our house:

Kids decide alone: How to act in school/Sunday school (Mom and Dad aren't around!).

Mostly a kid decision, with a little parent input: What to read, what TV to watch, choice of clothes, how to spend allowance.

Mainly a kid decision, but considerable parent input: Choice of friends, choice of dates in the future.

Joint decision: Planning a birthday party, taking in a foster child

God's will

DECISIONS

Proverbs 15:20-22

Kids decide alone

Kids and parents decide together

Parents decide alone

• how to act at school
• who to marry
• language
• choosing dates
• where to go to college
• how to act at Sunday School
• choosing friends
• buying a car
• family food
• memory verses

← inviting Keith →

• what to read—books, magazines
• choosing church clothes
• what TV to watch
• vacation details
• a pet
• choosing everyday clothes
• how much TV
• how to spend allowance
• planning birthday parties
• size of allowance
• playtime activities
• household tasks

(short-term). In the future, choosing a car, deciding whom to marry. (In our view, too many modern parents have assumed this last one is out of their territory. We wanted to serve notice early that we'd be expressing ourselves on that one! Not that we intend to dictate, but we will seek God's will along with our offspring.)

Major parent involvement, auxiliary kid input: What to wear to church; what Scriptures to memorize; where to go on vacation; eventually, choice of college.

Parents decide alone: Household tasks, size of allowances, how much TV, whether to have a pet, what language is acceptable.

The point here is to show graphically that not *everything* is over on the right side. Mom and Dad are not complete dictators after all. Some choices *have* been delegated.

Now comes a surprise. As you've been writing the various decisions on the chart across the left-right spectrum, *also place them vertically according to importance.* Don't announce what you're doing, but casually put "household tasks" near the bottom of the chart, "choosing friends" somewhere in the middle, "whom to marry" at the top, and so forth.

Then, take a yellow marker and shade in the top half or more of the field as you say, "Here are the decisions where God is likely to have an opinion about what we do. He probably doesn't care a whole lot about who is assigned to do the supper dishes. . . but he's very concerned about what we read and watch, how we behave, where we go to college, and so forth.

"In these areas, *both* kids and parents need to stop and find out what God thinks."

This visual spreadsheet will establish a lot of important parameters as children chase the golden ring of independence.

Where's Heaven?

Most kids are content to pass lightly over the subjects of death and heaven—until someone close to them dies. Then, suddenly, the questions sprout.

And they are not easy questions to handle, for the obvious reason that we haven't died or been to heaven! We can't speak from experience. The Scripture does give us some information, however, and we can pass it along to our children in the hours of grief. We don't need to plan a formal presentation; we're better off just responding to questions, Bible in hand.

"Where is heaven?"

This is a happy mystery; the Bible doesn't answer for sure. But wherever it is, we do know that God is there (see Gen. 28:17) and that Jesus speaks for us there (see Heb. 9:24).

"What do people do in heaven?"

It will probably be something like a great party! At least your favorite person will be there—Jesus—and you'll love him more than you can imagine. He'll be happy to see *you* so happy. You won't ever be sick or sad or tired. You won't get angry or jealous or upset.

What if you had a friend who'd never tasted pizza? Wouldn't it be hard to tell him or her how delicious it is? Describing heaven is sort of like that—it's beyond our words (see Rev. 21).

"Who gets to go to heaven?"

Everyone who has become part of Jesus' family (see John 3:16; Phil. 3:20-21).

"How come God took Aunt Rose to heaven even though we

prayed for her to get well?"

This is very hard to understand. But it's not quite accurate to say God took her away from us. The truth is this: Death took Aunt Rose—but Jesus has taken death! Jesus has already made her perfectly well again. She has never been happier, being right there with Jesus in her new body, which works better than her human body ever did (see 1 Cor. 15:49-51).

"When do we go to heaven?"

We don't know. Naturally, we think we'll live for a long time yet, and we probably will. But two things could happen to change that: (1) Death could take us earlier than we think; or (2) Jesus could come back! He said he's coming back to the earth for all his people someday. When? "In a flash, in the twinkling of an eye" (1 Cor. 15:52). That's pretty fast!

But the Bible doesn't say what day or hour. That's why we must be ready all the time. Just as we look forward to tulips and daffodils bursting out of the ground in the spring, we can look forward to Jesus' return (see 1 Thess. 4:16-18).

Our children have greatly appreciated the picture book *Heaven Has a Floor* by Evelyn Roberts (Damascus House), written by a grandmother for her grandson after both his parents were killed in a 1977 plane crash.

When the news came that a close friend of our family, a twenty-nine-year-old wife, had died following childbirth, our Tricia immediately went hunting the shelves for this book. It spoke quietly and steadily to her, and to us all, on that tragic morning. We were glad it was on hand.

After a Suicide

We were finishing a Monday morning breakfast, and Grace had just reminded Nathan to ask a friend about some detail when he quietly said: "I don't think he'll be in school today; his dad committed suicide last week. He shot himself in the bathroom."

Cereal spoons clanked to the table. *What?* The father of a good-natured boy who had played trombone alongside Nathan for four years had committed suicide right in the family home?

A newspaper account confirmed the grisly details. Our son had been asked by his friend to keep quiet and had done so until now.

Immediately our girls began a barrage of questions: "Why'd he do it?" "What are they going to do now?" "Is he in heaven?" We struggled under the shock until the kids left for school. Then we recognized that Home Together Night the following evening would have to deal with this serious matter. We had thirty-six hours to sort out our own feelings, do some research, and make some plans.

We hope you and your children never face a similar occasion, but if you do, here's one way to handle it. (We realize there are differences of opinion about whether one who takes his or her life forfeits eternal life, and we respect those differences. The following approach reflects our understanding of scriptural principle on this difficult subject.)

We gathered in a circle, and Dean began, "All right—what questions do you have about suicide?" The kids repeated the ones from the day before, especially the question about heaven.

"Well, life is a gift," he responded. "Actually, it's more like a loan from God. He gave it to us, he keeps it going, and he will end it. Obviously, we're not supposed to ruin something that isn't our own."

We stopped at this point to read Psalm 139:13-16 and

Colossians 1:15-17, Scriptures that make the above points.

"Now, you asked whether Mr. __________ is in heaven. Well, how do we get to heaven? How does anyone get to heaven?"

They answered properly, "By asking God to forgive you and take you into his family."

Dad: "Do we get to heaven by doing everything right?"

"No."

Dad: "We get to heaven because *Christ* did everything right. He's our 'ticket,' isn't he?

"So even though Mr. __________ did something horribly wrong last week—not only to himself but also to his wife and kids—whether he went to heaven or not was decided by whether he had trusted in Christ for salvation. Had he? I don't know.

"Yes, we should try to avoid doing wrong and should confess our sins to God when we do. But we're not kicked out of his family for misbehaving, any more than you're kicked out of this home for misbehaving."

Next issue: *Why would a person do such a thing?* "Well, some people who commit suicide know what they're doing, and they've decided everybody would be better off if they'd just get out of the way. They're very unhappy, maybe feeling unwanted or a bother, or maybe they're very angry at someone in their family, and this is kind of a revenge. They sometimes leave a note to explain or at least give hints about why they're killing themselves.

"Other people almost *don't* know why they do it. They're so confused, so irrational, or so on drugs that it's hardly a conscious decision at all." Here Dean told of one woman he'd read about who was observed carrying a quart jar of water in her car at all times "to take my pills" when sudden waves of panic would sweep over her. In her medicine cabinet were forty to fifty prescriptions from seven or eight different doctors. She eventually took her life.

"There are other reasons we probably don't understand yet. Even wise pastors and counselors and doctors are baffled sometimes."

Then we raised a new question to turn the conversation toward ministry: "How do you think the family is feeling right now?"

The children soon had a number of responses: sad, embarrassed, scared, angry, confused.

We felt we should do more than just talk about these people; we should reach out to them in some way. So we proposed a plan of action:

Grace and Nathan could take a casserole and plate of cookies, go knock on their door, say something like "We just want you to know we care about you"—and see what happened next.

Dean, Rhonda, and Tricia would stay home and pray for a successful contact.

As the three knelt by the couch, the girls expressed themselves to God very seriously and intently. It was a special time of intercession.

Meanwhile, across town, Grace and Nathan were welcomed inside the home with open arms. The wife and her parents-in-law had recently returned from the weekend burial in another state and were still trying to survey their shattered lives. The son promptly cornered Nathan to ask what he'd missed at school and to get help on some homework. Grace talked with the adults for a while and eventually left Nathan there for another hour to continue helping his classmate.

When a memorial service was held, Grace escorted Nathan and a carload of friends to attend. They also went to a home gathering afterward. The boy was included in Nathan's birthday party a couple of weeks later. Soon thereafter, the woman sold her home and moved her children closer to relatives, thus ending our active involvement. But in the time we had, we felt it was important to blend theology with compassion, thinking with doing, in the midst of this most painful tragedy.

Unlocking the Bible

If a child likes to read at all, sometime during the growing-up years he or she is going to take a crack at the Bible.

It will be thirty times more pages than he or she is used to. And there aren't any pictures (or not very many).

And some parts are less than thrilling.

How is the child to have a successful experience at Bible reading instead of a disappointment? Some simple guidance is in order.

Sit down with your children some evening and say, "Bible reading works a lot easier if you go at it using three simple questions:

1. "*What do these words say?* Are there any words here I don't understand? Should I use a dictionary, ask Dad, or what?
2. "*What does this mean?* What did it mean to the people who first read it? What was Jesus (or Paul, or whoever) trying to tell them?
3. "*What does this mean to me?* What is God trying to show *me* through this?"

Write this on a chalkboard, a piece of chart paper, or anything large. This three-point approach is the basis of most good inductive Bible study, for all ages.

Then, don't leave it at the theory level. Try it out.

"What book of the Bible have you been trying to read, Nikki? Let's do the next paragraph or chapter as a family."

Read the text together aloud (two verses each around the circle works fine). Then walk your way through the three questions. Remember, the first question deals with vocabulary and the factual part of the text. The second deals with what it all meant "back then." The third nails it home to us.

Finish by having everyone write these three questions in the front of their Bibles for future reference. And check from time to time on how people are getting along in their use.

Days to Remember

If your children were asked to name two times when God did something remarkable for *your* family, could they do it? Or for that matter, could you?

Through Scripture, there runs an underlying concern that the younger generation will forget—or never hear in the first place—about "the mighty works of God." The most striking example occurs when Israel crossed the Jordan River to begin the invasion of Canaan. The Lord had Joshua stop everything and appoint twelve men to pile up a monument of stones on the bank. Why? "To serve as a sign among you. In the future, when your children ask you, 'What do these stones mean?' tell them that the flow of the Jordan was cut off before the ark of the covenant of the Lord" (Josh. 4:6-7).

God ordered them to create something visual for the sole purpose of triggering questions from the kids. "Hey, Dad—what's that?" "Those rocks? Ah—let me tell you about the day God did something incredible for us. . ."

Every Christian family can start a notebook of "memorial stones"—occasions when God showed his love and care and power in a specific way. The longer you reminisce, the more things you'll recall that you *really don't* want to forget—things you want your children to know about and cherish along with you:

- The time you got that job you desperately needed and had prayed for.
- The time a long-resistant relative finally yielded to Christ.
- The time God healed someone in your family.
- The time God supplied a financial need in an unusual way.
- The time an unexpected award or honor came along.
- Maybe even how God spared a family member's life.

This may take more than one sitting, as strategic pieces of your family's walk with God are captured on paper.

Then, once the list is created, don't bury it. Bring it out a couple of times each year and add new entries. Every time you do, of course, you can also tell your children a story or two from the past, just as Israelite parents did . . . stories that will delight them and impress upon them that they belong to an *active* God.

Welcome to the Minority Group

Schoolteachers, politicians, and pastors may talk all they want about racial acceptance, but until parents show that they agree, children miss the point. What Dad and Mom say, the jokes they tell, and the ways they act in the presence of other races are more powerful than all the platitudes.

At our house in Illinois (a white home in a mostly white suburb), we welcomed the day when a black family moved in three doors down the street. Their kids were close in age to ours, and close friendships developed.

They considered our church but eventually decided to join a black church, where Rose became choir director. When she invited us to a musical drama, we were glad to accept. This would be an evening of good music plus a great learning experience for our children—if we laid some groundwork first. After all, when you're used to being the majority color, it can be a little unnerving to be suddenly in the minority.

The following approach can be used for any such occasion, not only visiting a minority church but going to a big city or any part of the country—or world—where your race is not dominant. These experiences are great for families and worth spending money to arrange.

The obvious Bible story for this occasion was Acts 10. In a circle, we read together how the Lord got Peter ready to go with just a few friends to be a handful of Jews in a houseful of Italians. Peter wasn't used to being in the minority. He was, in fact, quite against the idea. Staying with his own kind was a lot more comfortable.

But God said, in no uncertain terms, "Do not call anything impure that God has made clean" (v. 15).

Peter still wasn't thrilled, but eventually he had to admit, "I now realize how true it is that God does not show favoritism but accepts men from every nation who fear him and do what is right'' (vv. 34, 35). The trip turned out far better than Peter could ever have imagined, as Cornelius's whole family was converted, baptized, and filled with the Holy Spirit.

``When we go to Second Baptist tomorrow night,'' we told our children, ``a lot of things will be the same—it'll be regular 'church.' When Mrs. Haith leads her choir, you'll recognize some of the music. Some of it will be quite a bit different, though. And different people respond to music—and to the Lord—in different ways.

``That's okay. Don't spend the evening thinking about the differentness of this or that; just appreciate the service for what it is, without comparing it to something else.

``The other thing is this: we're going to be a few white dots in a sea of black faces. So what? That's how the Haiths feel on this street every day. Now the tables are turned. You can go on being yourself just as they do. Everybody in the church will be coming to honor the same Lord, and that's what binds us together.''

We enjoyed a marvelous evening, and near the end, when Rose Haith launched into a deep-soul solo, backed by her enthusiastic choir, our kids were mesmerized. The refreshments afterward in the fellowship hall provided us another chance to mix with ``the majority,'' greet and compliment our friends, and break stereotypes.

An appreciation for all God's people does not grow out of theory alone. It takes real-life contact to make kids understand what we mean.

Why Memorize?

Sooner or later it dawns on any church kid: Scripture memorization is work! Nathan was a seventh grader and had just under two hundred verses in his personal file box when he suddenly raised a normal junior-high question: "Why do we have to do this, anyway? What good is it?"

We rather insensitively brushed it aside a couple of times. But he kept raising the question until it dawned on us that we'd better respond.

The next Home Together Night, Grace adapted an idea she found in Wayne Rickerson's book *Getting Your Family Together.* Lighting two small candles, she turned out all the lights in the house and had us sit on the hard floor in a cramped corner of the kitchen between the table and the wall. "Imagine that we're a family in Ethiopia or Russia or one of the other countries that persecutes Christians," she began. "Imagine that we've been arrested and thrown into a prison cell with only the clothes on our backs. How would we pass the time?"

The kids suggested playing word games, trying to get some books to read, and doing calisthenics.

Next question: "What do you think would encourage us, keep us going, and keep us strong in spite of guards making fun of us, hurting us, or whatever?"

The answers eventually came around to the Bible, but, of course, we would have none in a Marxist prison. At that point, Grace produced small slips of paper and said, "But we have a hidden Bible—in our heads. Let's see how much we can write down."

For the next eight minutes, we wrote as many Scriptures as we could recall, one verse or set of consecutive verses per slip. Dean worked the Old Testament, the other four the New. Then we collated the papers in order. We talked about how much more we could re-create if we had *days* to think.

"But that's never going to happen here in our country," Nathan objected.

"We hope not," we replied. "But there's no guarantee. And who says you're going to spend your whole life in this country? God might want to use you in a dangerous place someday.

"And there are lots of times when we need God's truth at school or at work—and our Bibles are miles away. That's another reason why we carry it in our minds."

Dean finished off the "prison sentence" by telling about the first time his parents let him drive a car alone as a teenager to Wichita (thirty miles away) to hear John Noble, an American who had been imprisoned by the Soviets shortly after World War II. When the Christians in the camp gathered, Noble had said, they would not dare to sing. They merely *hummed* a tune such as "What a Friend We Have in Jesus." The guards paid little attention, but the believers went away greatly strengthened.

So we hummed two or three Scripture choruses—"They That Wait Upon the Lord," "Seek Ye First," "Finally, My Brethren, Be Strong in the Lord"—as a further use of "the hidden Bible."

A Taste of Sharing

Possessiveness is a chronic disease from the toddler stage straight through to puberty (and beyond?). "GIVE it to me! That's MINE." The infection is nationwide, it seems, with few children escaping the fever.

Thus, regular doses of teaching on the importance of sharing are called for. Sunday school teachers hit the theme often, but that is not enough. One simple approach for parents is to take a break between the evening meal and dessert for a homemade puppet show. You don't need lots of props: just a couple of decorated lunch bags over your hands, or colorful socks, or you can simply hold two stuffed animals, naming them Homer and Mabel. Ad-lib your own story about both of them wanting the same prized toy and launch into a horrendous brawl before it's over.

(Alternatives: One parent can do the puppeteering with an older child, or two older children can entertain the younger ones. For even greater effect, cut a rectangle out of the side of a refrigerator box to make a puppet theater.)

Will you feel a little silly? Of course. That's part of what makes it fun for your kids. They rarely get to see the ham in you, and they will pay attention.

Once the story reaches its peak, apply Romans 12:10 to the situation: "Be devoted to one another in brotherly love. Honor one another above yourselves." The King James Version says, "Preferring one another." Explore how Homer and Mabel might have responded differently.

Then say, "Okay—back to the table for dessert now." Without further comment, bring the ingredients for homemade sundaes. Only give Dad all the bananas, Kelly all the chocolate syrup, Jeff the whole carton of ice cream, someone else the whipped cream, and Mom the cherries. Provide each person with an empty bowl. The kids will get the message very quickly! If no one shares his or her ingredient, no one will get dessert.

Have fun "preferring one another" as you enjoy your sundaes.

You might want to insert a side discussion whether kids have to share all their cherished toys and dolls when Tommy the Tornado comes over to visit. One way to handle these cases is for kids to look around in advance and remove their breakables from Tommy's line of vision. That's not being possessive—just prudent!

Hiking Made Easy

Some kids (and parents) are avid hikers, while others have to be coaxed. We tend to be the second variety. But we managed a longer trek than we ever thought we could one summer evening by building in some mental enrichments.

The twins were only five years old at the time, and we weren't at all sure we could conquer the three-mile shoreline of a nearby lake. We took our dog along to give us something to chase. But what really made this outing work were lots and lots of rest stops.

We stopped to snack out of Mom's goodie bag (numerous times!).

We stopped several times to read a few pages from a book we'd been enjoying together at home.

We stopped to enjoy the scenery as the sun got low in the sky.

We stopped to sing "Here comes Jesus—see him walkin' on the water. . . ."

We stopped to watch a huge turtle making its way down the bank.

We stopped to memorize Philippians 4:8 (KJV), our verse for the night:

> Finally, brethren,
> whatsoever things are true,
> whatsoever things are honest,
> whatsoever things are just,
> whatsoever things are pure,
> whatsoever things are lovely,
> whatsoever things are of good report;
> if there be any virtue,
> and if there be any praise,
> think on these things.

We assigned each family member one of the adjectives (*true, honest,* etc.), and then turned the verse into a chant as we marched along, everyone belting out "Whatsoever things are—" and then waiting for the key word. By the time we got back to our car, we had the verse down cold!

That Scripture has remained our "hiking verse," and whenever we recite it or hear it mentioned in church, it brings back our own set of special memories about the night we walked around Blackwell Lake.

Beyond Sarcasm

In many families, sarcasm and put-downs have become an art. The adults are masters of verbal slash-and-burn, and so the children follow suit. Television comedy is a constant source of new scorchers as well. If Jeremiah lived in our generation, he might well say again, "Their tongue is a deadly arrow" (9:8a).

If, on the other hand, you want to create a home where safety prevails, where people can express themselves without risking a verbal karate chop, you have to work at it. You start by curbing your own bent for the delicious one-liner that leaves the other person in ribbons. That often requires considerable effort and personal prayer.

In many cases, the bite resides not so much in the words themselves as in the inflection, the slur, and the body language. But the damage is no less.

And as with breaking any other bad habit, it often helps to come up with a positive replacement. Kids justifiably wonder, "If I'm not supposed to say *that,* what *can* I say?" Give them an answer in the form of a chart:

NOT THE BEST	BETTER
"What a pity."	"I'm sorry you got hurt."
"Baloney."	"I don't think that's quite true."
"C'mon!"	"Could I please have that?"
"That's *your* problem."	[silence]
"You're *weird.*"	"That's unusual."
"Who *cares?*"	[silence]
"Aw*right*!" "Okay, Okay!"	"Okay."[pleasantly]
"You *would.*"	[silence]

"Shut up."	"Could you please not say that?"
"Well, I'm *so* sorry."	"I'm sorry."[normal tone]
"Copycat, copycat."	[ignore]

You can probably think of other stingers in your family's vocabulary that need disarming. Work out your own chart, post it for a week or two as a ready reference, and help each other find the better ways.

Why Our Goods Belong to God

How is a Christian child to catch the idea that our material possessions are not really ours—they're God's? Israelite children watched parents make repeated trips to the tabernacle or temple to present tangible items to Jehovah: animals, grain, money. The children watched returning armies hand over vast spoils to God in dedication.

It is far too easy for children and adults in our time to act like the rich fool in Jesus' story (see Luke 12:16-21) and assume our blessings are self-generated and therefore ours to control.

One way to combat this arrogance is to hold family dedication ceremonies whenever something major is acquired. These can be as simple as a five-minute time of prayer or as elaborate as a full evening with invited guests. We know a family that wrote an actual liturgy of thanksgiving for a new house, invited a dozen of us to come recite it with them, led us through the house for a statement of dedication in each room, and served refreshments! They really wanted God to know they considered this real estate his property, available for his use.

In our case, we've done more modest dedications of the following things:

- Each child's first musical instrument, and each upgrading thereafter.
- A home organ that was graciously given to us by Grace's uncle after her aunt passed away.
- A newly finished basement.
- A new car (followed by a family ride).

In each case, the prayers went something like this: "Father, we thank you for providing this. We're very happy to have it, but we acknowledge that it really belongs to you. We intend to use it for your purposes whenever we can. Help us not to abuse it. We want to have it always ready for your call. Again, we thank you, in Jesus' name. Amen."

Request Night

How many times in your life have you heard the story of David and Goliath? Plenty, right?

How many times has your first- or second-grader heard it? Twice? Probably not more than three times.

Parents often forget this difference. They also forget how much kids love their favorite stories repeated. And especially in the younger years, they need parental help in order to do this.

Hence, let us not be too sophisticated to sit down with younger children on family night and say, "Tonight, I'll read you any Bible story you want. You choose." Use an easy-to-understand translation, like the *Good News Bible.* And if they want to hear Noah and the ark, or Daniel and the lion's den, or Jesus rising from the dead, read it with as much freshness and excitement in your voice as if it were your first exposure.

Such are the moments of which memories are made.

The Request Night idea can be overused, of course, and can be the lazy way out for busy parents. But once every six months or so through the primary years, it's worthwhile.

How Many Rules?

Children sometimes think the world is swarming with do's and don'ts. Adults have thought up so many boundaries that you can hardly get out of bed in the morning without crossing one or another of them.

Really?

Start out some evening by asking, "How many rules do you think we have at our house? Take a guess." Write down everyone's number.

Next question: "Do you think God has lots of rules? How many?"

Then explain that the Pharisees thought so. They went through the Torah (first five books of the Old Testament) very carefully, making lists—and finally arrived at 248 do's and 365 don'ts. "That makes a total of how many?" (A little math drill here on the side . . .)

"But then Jesus came along and said, 'Wait a minute. All these lists give you the wrong impression of my Father. I can sum up all his rules in *two!*' "

Your kids may not believe you. Show them Matthew 22:34-40 (the two great commandments, which summarize "all the Law and the Prophets").

"That's really all God wants: for us to love him totally, and to love each other as much as we love ourselves. That takes care of everything!"

Then go on: "In the same way, we really don't have as many rules in our family as you might think."

At this point, you can either present a list you've drawn up or create one together with your children. The point is to keep it *short*, to show that what Dad and Mom require is not so overwhelming after all.

Your list will be unique to your parenting style and your values. When you finish, give it a catchy name, like "Paulson Principles" or "Smith Slogans." Then post it on the refrigerator or somewhere for repeated reference.

If you want some ideas for starters, here's our list. Try as we might, we couldn't come up with more than fifteen rules. We found it a great help to have the house policies spelled out on paper, succinctly, all on half a page.

MERRILL MOTTOES

1. No heaps!*
2. Take turns talking.
3. Be a gracious host.
4. Work first, play second. Don't wait for reminders about chores, music practice, and so forth.
5. Keep positive, not pouty.
6. Yelling is for emergencies only (when the house is on fire).
7. Speak with kindness, not sarcasm.
8. No attacks (hitting, kicking, slapping, tickling).
9. Mom or Dad must always know where you are.
10. Obey Dad, Mom, and those they put in charge.
11. Save water and electricity whenever you can.
12. Remember your phone phrases and table manners.
13. Keep outer doors closed in cold or hot weather (during heating or air conditioning).
14. Polite, reasonable questions are fine; back talk is not.
15. Be extra careful with other people's mail, keys, and change.

* piles of clothes left on the floor, bed or chair.

More than once this little code has proved helpful. Instead of making a big speech or harangue, we've simply quoted a line from the Mottoes (particularly 2, 4, 6, 9, and 14). The kids even use them on each other when it's to their advantage!

Meanwhile, the myth of the inexhaustible rulebooks (God's and parents') has been laid aside.

While You're Waiting in a Restaurant

Trying to keep young children pleasant in a restaurant while waiting for food is enough to ruin many a parental appetite. The greatest challenge, we think, is a pizza parlor. The half-hour wait can seen interminable.

Pencils from Mom's purse are fine until the paper napkins are used up. Then what? Dad's supply of jokes is usually not worth reviewing.

One night we decided to use these frustrating minutes for our teaching time. We brought along a three by five card for each child, passed out pencils, and had them write down a new memory verse: "Whatever you do, work at it with all your heart, as working for the Lord, not for men" (Col. 3:23).

Then we said, "Let's watch this waitress and see what kind of a worker she is. Study her; see whether she's really trying to meet our needs and desires. What kind of attitude does she show? Does she seem interested or bored? Do you think she's working with all her heart?"

The kids never took their eyes off her until the pizza arrived. Their half-whispered comments continued in a steady stream. "She was sure nice about bringing extra napkins." "How many tables does she have to take care of, anyway?" (Some realities about the work world were sinking in along the way.) "She has to stand up all the time, doesn't she? And yet she's not crabby." "Do you think she's a Christian?"

The waitress never knew she was being scrutinized. Her work, however, became an excellent model for three young future employees and their parents. Had she served poorly, of course, the teaching value would have been the same.

By the end of the meal, the children not only had the Scripture nailed down and ready to recite, but also had done an on-site study of its meaning. (And they'd stayed out of each other's hair until it was time to eat!)

How Does God Heal?

Most children in Christian homes send up a lot of requests about healing. Their brothers, sisters, moms, dads, grandmas, grandpas, and assorted other important people in their lives become sick, and they'd really like to see God make them well.

Sometimes these prayers are answered dramatically, sometimes more ordinarily, and sometimes they seem to be ignored. One Home Together Night when Grandpa Danielson was hospitalized and Rhonda was also facing a minor surgery, we talked together about this. "Each of you tell me what you'd do in these situations if you were the one sitting up there in heaven":

- "A teenager walks home from school in the winter without a jacket or gloves and gets a bad cold." The kids generally concluded that natural consequence would have to run its course.
- "A two-year-old twin falls off a bed and breaks her arm" (which had happened back in 1977). They remembered that healing had occurred inside a cast over a six-week period.
- "A drunk wakes up the next morning sick to his stomach. He asks God to make him well so he can go to work." Same as the cold situation above.
- "A mom gets bronchitis, and it won't go away for six months in spite of the doctor's prescriptions." (This too had happened. Only a stretch of daily prayer finally cured Grace's coughing fits).

We told some other stories of direct healings in our own experience, as well as some times when we were disappointed. The kids began to see that God has a variety of ways to respond to prayers for healing. And he may not always explain his reasons. But that doesn't mean we should give up asking for his help.

We took time to look at three Scriptures together:

- Exodus 15:26, where God clearly calls himself "the Lord who heals you."
- 2 Corinthians 12:7-10, where Paul tells how God didn't heal him but did give him the grace to endure his "thorn."
- Matthew 7:7-11, Jesus' positive invitation to "ask. . .seek . . .knock," secure in the knowledge that we're talking to a good Father in heaven who enjoys giving good gifts to his children.

Finally, we sang together "Silver and Gold Have I None (But Such as I Have Give I Thee)," the gospel song about the miracle of the lame man in Acts 3.

It is easy for adults to become cynical about subjects that sometimes baffle us. Such is the temptation about God's role in healing. But we are not called to explain everything, only to continue asking, expecting, trusting. And in his time, according to his perspective, he does all things well.

A Few Words About Dancing

Should Christian parents talk to their children about dancing?

(We may have just lost half the readers of this book! Some of you are probably saying, "Uh-oh. Legalism rears its ugly head. They're going to squash all the fun in life." While others are saying, "*Should* parents speak about this important issue? Of course. Don't these authors know dancing is a tool of the devil?")

We are, in fact, quite in favor of fun (and hope the rest of this book illustrates that). We are also in favor of identifying any current ploys of Satan to mess up our kids. If you share those two values, read on.

The issue for us is not body movement. It's not even watching others move their bodies. That's what attending a baseball game is all about. The human body is a creation of beauty and grace; it's nothing to be hidden or straitjacketed.

Then what *is* the issue? Why do we (and you?) feel uneasy watching some kinds of dancing? Are we simply hung up because of a Victorian past?

There is more to it than that. The issue, in our judgment, is *self-control,* the last of the nine fruits of the Holy Spirit (see Gal. 5:22-23). It is the fruit perhaps most hard to cultivate in children. They seem to exhibit love and joy almost effortlessly, along with frequent displays of peace, kindness, goodness, and gentleness. The battle to control themselves, on the other hand, is a long war.

That is why we sat down with our son and our particularly lithesome daughters one Home Together Night during the peak of the break-dancing craze and said, "Let's talk about dancing."

"Oh, no, Dad! We do this fun stuff in gym and it's okay, isn't it, please?"

We had done enough checking to be able to say, "Relax. We're not upset about anything you've been doing so far. We want to point out some things the Bible says so you'll have a basis for making decisions in the future."

We then opened our Bibles to the Galatians 5 passage mentioned earlier, followed by:

- 1 Thessalonians 5:5-8, which says, "Let us be self-controlled" *twice*.
- Titus 2:1-8, which prescribes self-control for "older men," "younger women," and "young men."

"Seems to me," Dean continued, "that some dancing is very self-controlled—and some isn't. Some is the total opposite of self-control. Can you think of examples of each?"

That wasn't hard. (We even got a few impromptu demonstrations.) Folk dancing and ballet were in one league, sensuous gyrating in quite another.

"Well, if God means for us to be self-controlled, not wild, we need to say no to some kinds of dancing, don't we? Anything that leads us toward wildness, toward loss of control, is out of bounds.

"The older you get, the more you'll be faced with some tough choices on this, and Mom and Dad won't always be there at that moment. That's why we wanted to nail this principle down tonight.

"It's good for kids, and it applies to adults, too. Sometimes on TV you see adults dancing, and while they're not particularly wild, the man and the woman are very close—and they're almost *never* husband and wife. So why are they acting as if they were married? They're edging toward losing control of their feelings, and then their bodies—and that's one of the things that breaks up marriages. That's why we believe ballroom dancing is out of bounds, too. You will never see your Mom or Dad caressing some other man or woman. We save that for one another.

"Not all Christians will agree with us on this, but we intend to stay on the safe side. So tuck this principle of self-control away and keep it for when you'll need it. And if at some point we feel we need to step in and say no to something you want to do, this is the basis on which we'll do it."

That sounded fair enough to the children, and so far, we are satisfied with how it has worked out. We haven't lived to the end of the parenting road yet, obviously, but our trust is in a timeless scriptural principle that rises above fads and personal preferences.

Better Books for Better Kids

How many Christian parents complain about their kids' reading material—without providing a wholesome alternative?

The answer is not, however, to hand Junior a Christian book and say, "Here, read this instead."

Far better to take a family trip to a Christian bookstore (hopefully one with a lively children's section) and announce before you walk in, "Everybody gets to pick out a new book tonight. Dad's buying."

Suddenly you've got the kids eager to find something they'll really read. The choice is theirs, but the option range is controlled by you (since you chose the store, and it's your money). That's what you call "Everybody wins."

When you return home, you might write on the flyleaf of each purchase, "Ordinary Day, October 13, 1988, from Mom and Dad." Then you'll probably want to curl up in front of the fire or some other cozy place to have Family Library Time the rest of Home Together Night.

Good, upbuilding literature is out there in the bookstores—if we just put the time, money, and priority into acquiring it. Our girls got started reading the Elizabeth Gail series by Hilda Stahl (Tyndale) this way and were so engrossed they kept buying the books with their own money.

The Christian bookstore is also the source of good family night games. "Seek," for example, is a Bible version of "Clue." There are now half a dozen different adaptations of Trivial Pursuit using Bible knowledge questions; make sure the one you buy is not too hard for children.

If your church has a library, stop there often with your children—and don't be in a hurry.

Sometimes they'll want to use these books for a school assignment. Tricia recently handed in a review of the biography *Fanny Crosby* by Ethel Barrett (Regal) and got an excellent response from her teacher. Another outstanding biography for kids is Barrett's *John Welch: The Man Who Couldn't Be Stopped* (Zondervan). It's the story of the feisty Scottish preacher and son-in-law of John Knox (father of Presbyterianism) who defied more than one king and dodged more than one cannonball.

At other times, ask your child to give a short oral summary of a recently read book during a family night. Nathan once kept us fascinated with a retelling of *Bruchko* (Creation House), the story of young Bruce Olson going all alone to live with the Motilone Indians of eastern Colombia and eventually bringing them to Christ. The good things about this approach are that the reader gets a chance to shine, and the rest of the family gets propagandized to read the book.

Pig-out Prevention

One of the tough lessons for many children in our part of the world is to learn self-control in the presence of an abundance of food. (Children in west Africa should be so harassed.)

It's one thing on ordinary days at mealtimes, with Mom limiting the size of servings. But when there's a family reunion potluck, a church smorgasbord, or a cookie-and-punch reception, kids are infamous for taking advantage.

Is this just a run-of-the-mill problem in parenting? Or is there any help to be gained from God's Word?

Two passages are relevant:

- John 6:25-27, which tells what happened *after* the feeding of the five thousand. A crowd of people chased Jesus to the other side of the lake—and he knew why. "Because you ate the loaves and had your fill," he said. "Do not work for food that spoils, but for food that endures to eternal life." In other words, he wasn't impressed with people who thought only about their stomachs.
- Proverbs 23:1-3, 19-21, which gives several good reasons not to be a glutton.

You can follow this up by saying, "Let's go around the circle and see what we've learned. Everybody finish this sentence: 'I shouldn't "pig out" because ________________.' "

Then, present some guidelines to keep in mind when lots of food is available:

- "How full am I? Do I really need more?"
- "Will there be enough for everyone?"
- "Am I being polite? How will it look if I go back to the table again?"

The final event of the night (to see whether the point has gotten across) is for Mom to bring out several tempting desserts, spread them out in glorious array, and then say, "Now, let's each choose just one"!

Don't be surprised if family members keep reminding one another of this teaching at crucial moments in the future. That's all right; we all need help.

Singing from the Original

The abundance of Scripture music over the last fifteen years has been a fresh breeze to the church. It has reminded us that the Psalms—and other portions as well—were originally the lyrics of God's singing people.

To make this clear to children, try singing *and referencing* as many Scripture choruses as you can. If someone in your family plays the piano, guitar, or autoharp, use his or her talents; otherwise, just sing without accompaniment. With a Bible in each lap, look up the texts as you go along.

Where will you find them? Below is a partial list, but you'll probably need a concordance, too. This is a great opportunity to show your children the advantages of such a reference tool.

(No concordance at your house? Consider investing nineteen to twenty-three dollars for an unabridged one. That's less than a year's subscription to *TV Guide* and will do your family twice as much good.)

The Lord will fight for you	Exod. 14:14
I will sing unto the Lord	Exod. 15:1-2
The joy of the Lord is my strength	Neh. 8:10
I will call upon the Lord	Ps. 18:3, 46
The law of the Lord is perfect	Ps. 19:7-10, 14
Surely goodness and mercy	Ps. 23:6
Unto thee, O Lord, do I lift up my soul	Ps. 25:1-2, 4
The Lord is my light	Ps. 27:1
I will bless the Lord at all times	Ps. 34:1-4
Clap your hands, all ye people	Ps. 47:1
Great is the Lord	Ps. 48:1-2
Create in me a clean heart	Ps. 51:10

Thy lovingkindness is better than life	Ps. 63:3-4
I will sing of the mercies of the Lord	Ps. 89:1
I exalt thee	Ps. 97:9
Make a joyful noise unto the Lord	Ps. 100
I will enter his gates	Ps. 100:4
Bless the Lord, O my soul	Ps. 103:1
From the rising of the sun	Ps. 113:3
This is the day	Ps. 118:24
I was glad when they said unto me	Ps. 122:1
Come, bless the Lord	Ps. 134:1-2
Search me, O God	Ps. 139:23-24
Praise ye the Lord	Ps. 150
His name shall be praised	Prov. 18:10
I am my Beloved's and he is mine	Song of Sol. 6:3; 2:4
They that wait upon the Lord	Isa. 40:31
Therefore the redeemed of the Lord	Isa. 51:11
Our God reigns	Isa. 52:7
He was wounded for our transgressions	Isa. 53:5
He gave me beauty for ashes	Isa. 61:3
Put on the garment of praise	Isa. 61:3; 1 Cor. 14:15
The Lord thy God in the midst of thee	Zeph. 3:17
Not by might, not by power	Zech. 4:6
Our Father, which art in heaven	Matt. 6:9-13
Seek ye first	Matt. 6:33
I am the resurrection and the life	John 11:25-26
A new commandment	John 13:34-35
This is my commandment	John 15:11-12
Silver and gold have I none	Acts 3:6, 8
If that same Spirit	Rom. 8:11
We are heirs of the Father	Rom. 8:17
One body, one Spirit	Eph. 4:4-5
Making melody in your heart	Eph. 5:10
Finally, my brethren, be strong	Eph. 6:10-11

He is Lord	Phil. 2:10-11
Rejoice in the Lord always	Phil. 4:4
The fullness of the Godhead	Col. 2:9-10
In everything give thanks	1 Thess. 5:16-20
Now unto the King eternal	1 Tim. 1:17
Come and worship, royal priesthood	1 Pet. 2:9
Thou art worthy	Rev. 4:11
Alleluia, for the Lord Thy God . . .	Rev. 19:6-7

Even better than at home, use this idea in the car. It will make fifty or a hundred miles simply evaporate.

Many of the above, and others as well, can be found in the Benson Co.'s *Scripture in Song* Series. Individual titles are *Songs of Praise* (I and II), *Songs of the Kingdom* (I and II), *Songs of Joy,* and *Best of Scripture in Song.* There are also *Psalms Alive* (I and II) from Maranatha and Christine Wyrtzen's *Critter Country* from Multnomah.

In Concert, Live!

One of the griefs about piano lessons (as forty million children will testify) is that they're so much work and so little glory.

Parents can do something about that. Home Together Night is a perfect opportunity to showcase a child's accomplishments to a small but appreciative audience. Several times a year, psych up your young student to perform his or her best for the rest of the family.

As a matter of fact, why not go the whole route and invite guests in for a home recital? Grandparents, aunts, uncles, perhaps another family who might be asked to dinner—they'll all smile and applaud and make the budding musician(s) feel marvelous.

Have your children make programs for each guest. If you're serving cake for dessert, decorate it with musical notes and buy some special napkins for the occasion.

One thing many Christian parents don't realize is that they *can* influence the choice of repertoire piano teachers use. (After all, who's footing the bill?) Our children can learn to play more than "The Blue Danube" and "Theme from Star Wars." Go ahead and place an order at the Christian bookstore for some piano books of your child's approximate mastery level; then pass them along to the teacher with a polite request for consideration. You may wind up with a song worthy of performing in church.

Most religious retailers won't have what you're looking for on the shelf; you'll need to place a special order. This is even more true if your child is studying an orchestral instrument (brass, woodwind, string). But it's worth the effort and the wait. There *are* quality Christian music scores on the market; you just have to do a little digging through the bookstore's file of catalogs.

One more thing: when you have a home recital, don't forget to tape-record it. In fact, set aside a cassette for each of your children, and keep adding to it throughout the years. Preface each segment with a dateline announcement ("Now it's December 28, 1988, and Jennifer is in fourth grade. She's going to play two songs today. . . ."). The more you develop an "audio scrapbook," the more both you and the child will cherish it in years to come. From preschool days on, make this a priority.

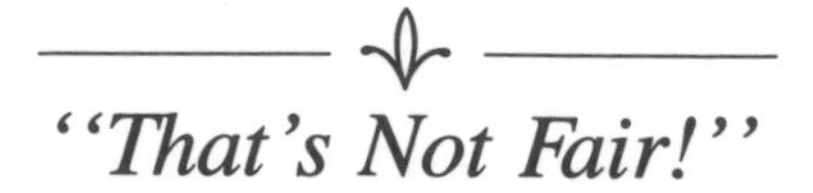

"That's Not Fair!"

A young person's greatest obsession some weeks seems to be with fairness. The debate rages on a hundred different fronts, from who got to ride in the front seat last, to who got to stretch his bedtime more, to who got a dessert three milligrams larger than someone else. The problem is not always that somebody got cheated; it's that somebody *else* allegedly got a windfall!

One February night when we were nearing exhaustion with such goings-on, Dean read to the family the following account by Robert De Moor; it had appeared in a magazine called *The Banner:*

> Back in Ontario when the apples ripened, Mom would sit all seven of us down, Dad included, with pans and paring knives until the mountain of fruit was reduced to neat rows of filled canning jars on the basement shelf. She never bothered to keep track of how many we did, though we younger ones undoubtedly proved to be more a nuisance than a help: cut fingers, squabbles over who got which pan, apple core fights. But regardless of our output, the reward for everyone was always the same: the largest chocolate-dipped cone money could buy. A stickler might argue that it wasn't quite fair, since the older ones actually peeled apples. But I can't remember anyone ever complaining about it. A family understands that it operates under a different set of norms than a courtroom does. In fact, when my younger brother had to make do with a popsicle because the store ran out of ice cream, we all felt sorry for him despite his lack of productivity (he'd eaten all the apples he'd peeled that day—both of them).

The kids were adequately charmed at that point. Next we turned together to Matthew 20:1-16, the parable of the workers in the vineyard. Dean explained how farm workers in Palestine would stand around a certain place waiting to be hired for the day, and how one denarius was about an average day's pay. Then we read the story aloud.

The questions were obvious enough:

- "Did the first workers have a legitimate gripe? Did the landowner keep his word or not?"
- "Then why did they throw such a fit?"
- "Does God have a right to be 'too generous' if he feels like it?"
- "Does Dad? Does Mom?"
- "What's the best response when somebody else gets a break?"

We let Jesus' rather clever story do its own work and simply plugged the appropriate passage of Scripture into our life experience.

(If you think we laid this problem to rest for good around our house, you're a dreamer. But we made some progress on it.)

The Bible and the Zoo

Why do children love the zoo so much? Because they're in love with life—all forms (even reptiles!). Children the world over are fascinated with the luxuriant variety of created beings. While major zoos usually require a day-long excursion, many areas have smaller wildlife preserves, animal shelters, park district rehabilitation centers where injured animals or birds are nursed back to health, and children's farms that are just the right size for a Home Together Night trip. Town families often have farming friends who would be glad to show visitors around the feed lot and let them explore the haymow along with the kittens.

Christian parents have a special addition to make to these outings: the news that the Lord God made all these wonderful colors and diversity and that he cares about the many needs of animals. He shows how much he knows about zoology in his major pronouncement to downcast Job (starting with 38:39 and running all the way through chapter 41). Here he treats us to an amazing display of facts about the lion, mountain goat, doe and fawn, wild donkey, wild ox, ostrich, stork, horse, hawk, eagle, "behemoth" (probably the hippopotamus or elephant), and "leviathan" (probably the crocodile). In fact, this last beast gets an entire chapter.

Any section of this makes a great family reading before or after a trip to the zoo, or perhaps during a rest break. Proverbs 30:24-31 is another good selection, with its four small but wise creatures (ants, conies or rock badgers, locusts, lizards) and its three "stately" things (the lion, the strutting rooster, and the he-goat).

Such reading enhances a child's wonder at such a creative, awesome God. It connects real, tangible surroundings with their Source.

Homemade Helpers

Two of the perennial enjoyments of the grade-school years—jigsaw puzzles and word searches—can be put to just about any use you want, depending on your teaching theme. Word searches (in case you've been an adult too long) are those mystifying batteries of alphabet soup in which real words lurk—if you can keep from going cross-eyed long enough to find them. Most kids can. Example:

FRUIT OF THE SPIRIT
Galatians 5:22-23 (NIV)

```
G P R P E A C E L Y Z A
H A G S S E N D O O G B
E T R E V E M I V J D O
K I N D N E S S E B W K
S E L E B T C O B D A P
B N U C E C L Z N E L B
O C O G F V R E S O V E
T E Y H C A E P N V K I
L O R T N O C F L E S X
F A I T H F U L N E S S
Q U O K M I D Z E J L S
```

What most parents don't stop to realize is that they *don't* have to buy these in a book somewhere; kids love to make up their own. (The above one took about fifteen minutes.) All you do is (1) choose a theme; (2) plot the words on an open sheet of paper or posterboard, interlocking them as much as you can and making some go diagonally, backwards, and bottom-to-top just to be ornery; (3) fill in the rest of the squares with unnecessary letters.

A parent can prepare one of these ahead of Home Together Night, making photocopies for each family member. Or you can sit down as a family at one time and each person make a word search for someone else.

Possible themes are "Old Testament Heroes," "New Testament Heroes," "What Makes a Loving Home," and "Things I Like." Once everyone is finished, trade papers and start searching.

When it comes to puzzles, just about any large picture from a Sunday school paper or teaching packet can be used. Once again, make your own—or let kids make their own.

1. Paste the picture onto a piece of cardboard.
2. Flip it over and draw lines at random, like a puzzle.
3. Cut along the lines.
4. Store in a Ziploc bag or small box for repeated use.

The same thing can be done with any section of Scripture you want to emphasize or memorize. One night at the beginning of a school year, we printed Romans 12:14, 17, 18, 21 (a great passage on getting along with non-Christians) on orange posterboard, then cut it into a jigsaw puzzle. As particular verses became apparent, we discussed the passage's main ideas.

The Pinocchio Principle: Lying

Children of all ages continue to be charmed with the story of the puppet-come-to-life who helps his master but then goes astray by fudging on the truth. The movie version of *Pinocchio* makes the rounds every few years in either theaters or on television, and it's also now available to VCR owners in videocassette form.

Meanwhile, picture books are waiting at virtually every public library.

When the movie came to our town, we decided to have a Pinocchio night. A doll of the little fellow with his nose already lengthening served as the table centerpiece. Before we left for the movie, we passed out slips of paper with Scriptures to look up: the Ninth Commandment (Exod. 20:16); Psalm 34:12-13; Proverbs 19:5, 9, 22; Ephesians 4:25; Colossians 3:9-10; 1 John 2:21-22; Revelation 21:8. The Bible is rather clear on this subject!

"Why do you think God makes such a big deal of telling the truth?" Dean asked. "Because he knows—as Mom and I know—that if we can't trust what each other says here in our home, everything else breaks down. We'd all have to go around checking on each other to see whether the other person was lying or not. It's terribly time-consuming, and it also produces all kinds of worry and suspicion.

"We have *got* to be able to know that whatever comes out of my mouth, your mouth, his mouth, and her mouth is for real. The same goes for school, for work, for our town, for our nation. Whenever we can't believe each other, we're in real trouble."

He then told about his grandparents on both sides, all but one of whom were raised in the Society of Friends (Quakers). "They had a saying that went like this: 'A Quaker's word is as good as his bond.' In other words, if he said something, it was as sure as if he had offered money to prove it. He didn't need to say 'I bet you' or anything extra; he was a Christian who never lied, and that was enough. And in our family today, we're continuing that tradition."

Soon the discussion was over, and we were off to the theater for a cartoon reinforcement of the same idea.

Parallel Parables

"Tonight we're going to read a certain Bible story, but you have to figure out which one," we announced one evening. "Your clue will be this song."

We then played Ken Medema's subtle, intriguing "Mr. Simon," from his cassette *Lookin' Back* (Word), which is a creative recasting of the parable of the Pharisee and the tax collector. The kids soon recognized the source, and we turned together to Luke 18:9-14. (This approach can be used with other stories as well, as Christian musicians—particularly Don Francisco—create more and more of these ballads.)

We then proceeded with a simple kid-level Bible study:

1. Was the Pharisee *doing* anything wrong in his life?
2. Then what was his problem?
3. Why do you think the tax collector stood in the back?
4. Why is it so hard for us to confess?
5. What kind of attitude is God looking for?
6. Let's retell this story as if it had happened at *our* church. First, a grown-up version, then a kid version.

Imaginations went to work, and soon we had created two colorful takeoffs. (This is one method educators use to ingrain a principle or truth in students' minds: have them translate it into a different form from the original. The mulling over, which such an effort requires, makes the idea stick.)

In this parable, of course, the main idea is superb for us all: boastfulness doesn't impress God, even if we boast about worthy things. He is far more interested in reaching down to the humble.

Pushing and Pulling Against God

A common metaphor among us parents is the idea of *molding* or *shaping* young lives. We often use the language of ceramics to describe our task: working with pliable personalities to create attractive, well-adjusted adults.

But even greater than this is the truth from Scripture that *God shapes us all.* He is the ultimate potter, working on lumps of human clay both young and old.

Children need to know we *all* come under his skillful thumb at times. They can readily understand this message from Jeremiah 18:1-6, the prophet's trip to the potter's house.

A good way to set the stage is to make homemade modeling clay together. Here's a recipe we got from a reliable source: a nearby nursery school! It works great.

2 cups flour
½ cup salt
2 cups water
2 tablespoons oil
2 tablespoons cream of tartar
Food coloring (your choice)

Stir together at low temperature with a wooden spoon, until the mixture thickens to the right consistency. Then knead it on a floured surface. That's all it takes.

Your children will enjoy this process (and once again, you've showed them that not everything has to come ready-made from a store). While you're kneading and then playing with the clay, read the Jeremiah story. The application is direct enough: that God is like a great potter or ceramics expert, and he shapes us the way he knows best.

The only trouble is, sometimes his clay gets stubborn. It fights back.

"How would you feel, Tara, if your lump of clay there started pushing back against your hand? What if it even talked back and said, 'But I don't *want* to be a ball! I want to be a dog instead!' What would you do?

"You'd probably say, 'Look—who made you on the stove just a little while ago?!'

"That's exactly what God says in verse 6: 'O house of Israel, can I not do with you as this potter does? . . . Like clay in the hand of the potter, so are you in my hand.' Our job is to cooperate and let God shape our lives, our attitudes, our actions, everything about us in whatever way he decides. After all, he knows what he's doing.

"And that goes for us grown-ups as well as kids." Dad might want to follow this statement with an example from his own life, which will probably inspire the children to add a few of their own.

(Store your homemade clay in a plastic bag inside a coffee or shortening can. When it starts getting old and crumbly, add a little water and let it sit overnight. Then work with it the next day.)

A similar point can be illustrated by a good old-fashioned tug-of-war in the yard or a park. Establish a center line (a sidewalk, a baseball bat, somebody's jacket), and divide into teams on opposite ends of a strong rope, an old garden hose, or even a no-longer-needed bedsheet or blanket (twisted for strength). Mom plus the kids can usually overpower Dad struggling alone, which is a huge delight for everyone (provided Dad's a good sport). Or you can arrange the teams in other creative ways.

Go through as many rounds as you can take, and then collapse on the ground together. While you're resting, say, "I have a couple of verses to read. See if you can find the connection between our tug-of-war and what this says."

"[God says:] 'I will instruct you and teach you in the way you should go; I will counsel you and watch over you. Do not be like the horse or the mule, which have no understanding but must be controlled by bit and bridle or they will not come to you' " (Ps. 32:8-9).

"A man who remains stiff-necked after many rebukes will suddenly be destroyed—without remedy" (Prov. 29:1).

"Submit yourselves, then, to God. Resist the devil, and he will flee from you. Come near to God and he will come near to you. . . . Humble yourselves before the Lord, and he will lift you up" (James 4:7-8, 10).

You might ask your kids, "What if God were on one end of the rope? Who would win?"

Then add, "Does God always use his power to make us obey?"

Help your children realize that God doesn't like having to jerk and pull against our resistance. He's strong enough to overpower us, and he will, if necessary. But how much better to let him lead us with ease.

Company Night

As mentioned in the opening chapter, not every Home Together Night needs to be "just us." It's occasionally enriching to invite guests to join you—IF the evening can remain child-centered. If all adults can accept this as an evening to key into the children, not to drift into adult conversation, a great deal can be modeled about Christian fellowship and outreach.

One evening we invited a family close to us to share our Home Together Night meal. Their daughter occasionally baby-sat for us, and their son was Nathan's age. After dessert, we brought out Bibles and said, "Now we're going to see what the New Testament has to say about relating to 'each other' or 'one another.' Here's a Scripture for each of you to look up.

"Once you find your verse, then think of a way you could carry it out toward someone in this room—in either family. Be practical: what does the Bible verse mean *for you to do?*"

Here were the Scriptures we used:

• John 15:17	"Love each other."
• Rom. 12:10	"Be devoted to one another in brotherly love."
• Rom. 15:7	"Accept one another."
• 1 Cor. 12:25	"Have equal concern for each other."
• Gal. 5:13	"Serve one another in love."
• Eph. 4:32	"Be kind and compassionate to one another."
• Eph. 5:21	"Submit to one another."
• 1 Thess. 4:18	"Encourage each other."
• James 5:16	"Confess your sins to each other and pray for each other so that you may be healed."

The ways to implement the Scripture ranged from "Help my sister make her bed" to "Give a compliment a day" to "Take time to see you after church and find out how your week has gone." Our sense of appreciation for each other and bonding seemed to increase the longer we talked. There were those smiles of affection and gratitude that seldom blossom in other circumstances.

The two families then played the Bible game "Seek" as a further expression of our "one-anotherness."

The Fine Art of Choosing Right from Wrong

Right vs. wrong: children meet the two categories early in life. They are expected to choose one, reject the other. And they sincerely want to (most of the time). But how?

One Home Together Night we simply handed everybody a blank sheet of paper and said, "Draw a situation in your life where you have to choose between right and wrong."

Tricia drew herself in the middle with a pleasant-looking girl holding a ball on one side and two rather mean-faced girls on the other. She titled it, "Choosing my friends."

Rhonda drew herself in pajamas, sick, and Mom holding a spoon and medicine. The dilemma: whether to cooperate and swallow the stuff or not.

Nathan drew himself at a school desk taking a test, to represent the temptation to cheat.

Grace drew herself at a table with her Bible. Then came the big word "OR," and on the other side was a grocery store, the garden, a telephone, and four other distractions that try to pull her away from her devotional life.

Since it was early springtime, Dean drew himself at a desk with financial records, a calculator, and Form 1040 in front of him.

Each person held up his or her picture and explained the choice between right and wrong. Then we said, "How do we make these choices? Let's each come up with one helpful guideline."

By the time we'd written all five contributions on the bottom of our drawings, we were pleased with the results. In our case, they turned out to be:

- *Think what Jesus would do.*
- *Think about the results* [what will take place following your decision one way or the other].

- *Pray for help in deciding.*
- *Know what the Bible says about this* [or find out].
- *Talk it over with parents, pastors, or other leaders.*

Your family's conclusions may emerge in quite different words. The exercise of posing specific right/wrong choices and talking about how to handle them, however, is bound to help your family in the future.

First Communion

Most young Christians' first approach to the Lord's table occurs during the grade-school years. In many churches, a catechism study or other coursework must precede such a step; others have no such rule. In some churches, a minimum age is specified, while others trust parental discretion.

Regardless of structure or its absence, this *is* a big event, and a little home reinforcement of its meaning can't hurt.

Here's a multiple-choice quiz Dean and Nathan (then in junior high) put together for Rhonda and Tricia (then beginning fourth grade) as their first experience of Communion drew near.

COMMUNION QUIZ

1. When God was getting the Israelites out of Egypt, he used ten great disasters to convince Pharaoh. The last one was:
   a. Plague of flies
   b. Plague on the firstborn
   c. Plague on the frogs
   d. I need to see the verses (Exod. 11:4-8)
2. The Israelites protected themselves from this disaster by:
   a. Spreading blood on the doorposts
   b. Praying all night
   c. Putting food outside
   d. I need to see the verse (Exod. 12:7)
3. That's why this holiday came to be known as:
   a. Thanksgiving
   b. Passover
   c. St. Patrick's Day
   d. I need to see the verses (Exod. 12:26-27)

4. Inside their homes that night, the Israelites:
   a. Went to bed and hoped for the best
   b. Watched television
   c. Ate lamb, bitter herbs, and bread
   d. I need to see the verse (Exod. 12:8)
5. To take part in this special night, you had to:
   a. Be circumcised (if you were male)
   b. Be hungry
   c. Be willing to see a lamb killed
   d. I need to see the verses (Exod. 12:48-49)
6. In the New Testament, Jesus and his disciples felt this holiday was:
   a. An old tradition you could forget about now
   b. Optional, if you really want to observe it
   c. Still an important part of serving God
   d. I need to see the verses (Matt. 26:17-18)
7. Then Jesus changed the holiday by drawing attention to two new ideas. The flat bread, he said, would now be a symbol of: *(alternate wording—"would now become:")*
   a. The Bible, which feeds us
   b. His broken body, soon to be crucified
   c. God's goodness in giving us our daily bread
   d. I need to see the verse (Matt. 26:26)
8. The drink would be a symbol of: *(alternate wording—"would become:")*
   a. God's goodness in giving us liquids to drink
   b. His blood, which would be spilled to pay for our sins
   c. The Red Sea, split by a miracle when the Israelites left Egypt
   d. I need to see the verses (Matt. 26:27-28)
9. Whenever the disciples had Communion in the future, Jesus said they should:
   a. Be in church
   b. Sing and worship the Lord

c. Remember him

d. I need to see the verse (Luke 22:19)

10. Circumcision in the Old Testament was an outward sign that you belonged to God. What's the equal sign now that tells who you are?

a. Water baptism

b. Going to church

c. Carrying a Bible

d. I need to see the verses (Col. 2:11-12)

11. If Old Testament believers had to be circumcised before eating the Passover, should we be baptized before receiving Communion?

a. Yes

b. No

c. Doesn't matter

d. I don't know

12. Paul scolded the Corinthian church for doing what at Communion time?

a. Skipping it

b. Thinking only of themselves

c. Using the wrong food

d. I need to see the verses (1 Cor. 11:20-22a)

13. What does Paul tell us to do before Communion?

a. Sing and worship

b. Listen to a sermon

c. Check ourselves for sin, and confess what we find

d. I need to see the verses (1 Cor. 11:28, 31-32)

14. In light of 1 Corinthians 11:33-34, why do we not let little kids take Communion?

a. They might spill something

b. They'd think mainly about getting to eat

c. They're in children's church instead

d. I need to see the verses (1 Cor. 11:33-34)

This quiz works fine as a paper-and-pencil exercise, followed by the child and parent sitting down together to talk through the answers and clear up any uncertainties.

We are aware of the doctrinal differences among churches regarding Communion; that is why we included the alternate words for questions 7 and 8. Use whatever is consistent with your beliefs and make any other changes you find necessary. Questions 10 and 11 relate specifically to churches that practice believer's baptism. The questions press the analogy that as circumcision preceded Passover, water baptism (our declaration that we are Christ's) should precede coming to his table. This is a conviction of ours; but again, if it is not yours, you may want to delete the section.

In our case, Nathan programmed the quiz into the home computer, complete with beeps for correct answers, flashes of "How about looking at the verses?" for incorrect answers, the Scripture references available when called for (option D), and a score at the end. The girls enjoyed the technological touch but also asked a number of clarifying questions about the content—which was what we wanted to occur.

If you're interested, here's the program in BASIC. Be our guests.

```
 5  HOME
10  REM COMMUNION
15  FLASH
17  VTAB 10: HTAB 16
19  PRINT "COMMUNION"
21  VTAB 13: HTAB 19
23  PRINT "QUIZ"
25  NORMAL
27  VTAB 23:HTAB 7: PRINT "by Dean and Nathan Merrill"
29  FOR A = 1 TO 1250: NEXT A
30  HOME
34  A = 1
36  DIM B$(7)
46  T = 0: ONERR   GOTO 250
47  IF A = 11 THEN FOR B = 1 TO 6: READ B$(B): NEXT B: GOTO 52
48  FOR B = 1 TO 7: READ B$(B): NEXT B
52  PRINT "QUESTION NUMBER";A;".": PRINT
56  PRINT B$(1);" ";B$(2)
60  PRINT : PRINT
68  PRINT "(A) ";
72  HTAB 5
76  PRINT B$(3)
84  PRINT "(B) ";
```

```
88   HTAB 5
92   PRINT B$(4)
100  PRINT "(C) ";
104  HTAB 5
108  PRINT B$(5)
112  PRINT"(D) ";
116  HTAB 5
118  IF A = 11 THEN PRINT "I don't know.": GOTO 128
120  PRINT "I want to see the verses."
128  PRINT : PRINT "YOUR CHOICE?";: GET N$: PRINT N$
129  IF N$ = "A" THEN B = 1
130  IF N$ = "B" THEN B = 2
131  IF N$ = "C" THEN B = 3
132  IF N$ = "D" THEN B = 4
136  IF B$(6) = "A" THEN 148
140  IF B$(6) = "B" THEN 152
142  IF B$(6) = "C" THEN 156
148  ON B GOTO 168,192,192,204
152  ON B GOTO 192,168,192,204
156  ON B GOTO 192,192,168,204
160  HOME
164  GOTO 52
168  PRINT : PRINT
172  PRINT : PRINT
176  INVERSE
180  HTAB 18: PRINT CHR$ (7); CHR$ (7); CHR$ (7); "RIGHT!!!!"
182  FOR V = 1 TO 500: NEXT V
184  NORMAL
186  IF T = 0 THEN S = S + 1
188  A = A + 1: HOME : GOTO 46
192  IF A = 11 AND N$ = "B" THEN 188
193  IF A = 11 AND N$ = "C" THEN 188
195  PRINT : PRINT
196  PRINT "HOW ABOUT LOOKING AT THE VERSES?";
200  PRINT
204  IF A = 11 AND N$ = "D" THEN 188
208  PRINT : PRINT "THE REFERENCE IS ";B$(7);"."
210  T = 1
224  VTAB 23
228  PRINT "HIT THE SPACE BAR WHEN YOU ARE"
232  PRINT "FINISHED READING. ";
236  GET Z$
240  HOME
244  GOTO 52
250  HOME
254  PRINT "THAT'S ALL THE QUESTIONS."
258  PRINT "YOU GOT "S" OUT OF 14 ON THE FIRST TRY."
262  IF S>10 THEN 274
270  PRINT "NOT TOO GOOD. YOU SHOULD TRY IT AGAIN."
272  GOTO 278
274  PRINT "THAT'S PRETTY GOOD."
276  PRINT "YOU'RE READY FOR COMMUNION."
278  PRINT : PRINT : PRINT
280  PRINT "BYE!!!!!!!!!!!!!!!!!"
285  END
300  DATA "When God was getting the Israelites out of Egypt, he used"
302  DATA "ten great disasters to convince Pharaoh. The last one was:"
304  DATA "Plague of flies","Plague on the firstborn","Plague of the frogs"
306  DATA "B","Exodus 11:4¢8"
308  DATA "The Israelites protected themselves from this disaster by:"
310  DATA "","Spreading blood on the doorposts","Praying all night"
312  DATA "Putting food outside","A","Exodus 12:7"
```

```
314 DATA "That's why this holiday came to be known as:";""
316 DATA "Thanksgiving";"Passover";"St. Patrick's Day"
318 DATA "B", "Exodus 12:26–27"
320 DATA "Inside their homes that night, the Israelites:";""
322 DATA "Went to bed and hoped for the best";"Watched television"
324 DATA "Ate lamb, bitter herbs, and bread";"C";"Exodus 12:8"
326 DATA "To take part in this special night, you had to:";""
328 DATA "Be circumcised (if you were a male)";"Be hungry"
330 DATA "Be willing to see a lamb killed";"A"; "Exodus 12:48–49"
332 DATA "In the New Testament, Jesus and his disciples felt this"
334 DATA "holiday was:";"An old tradition you could forget about now"
336 DATA "Optional, if you really want to observe it"
338 DATA "Still an important part of serving God";"C";"Matthew 26:17–18"
340 DATA "Then Jesus changed the holiday by drawing attention to two new"
342 DATA "ideas. The flat bread, he said, would now be a symbol of:"
344 DATA "The Bible, which feeds us";"His broken body, soon to be crucified"
346 DATA "God's goodness in giving us our daily bread";"B";"Matthew 26:26"
348 DATA "The drink would be a symbol of:";""
350 DATA "God's goodness in giving us liquids to drink"
352 DATA "His blood, which would be spilled to pay for our sins"
354 DATA "The Red Sea, split by a miracle when the Israelites left Egypt"
356 DATA "B";"Matthew 26:27–28"
358 DATA "Whenever the disciples had Communion in the future, Jesus said"
360 DATA "they should:";"Be in church";"Sing and worship the Lord"
362 DATA "Remember him";"C", "Luke 22:19"
364 DATA "Circumcision in the Old Testament was an outward sign that you"
366 DATA "belonged to God. What's the equal sign now that tells who you are?"
368 DATA "Water baptism";"Going to church";"Carrying a Bible";"A"
370 DATA "Colossians 2:11-12"
372 DATA "If Old Testament believers had to be circumcised before eating the"
374 DATA "Passover, should we be baptized before receiving Communion?"
376 DATA "Yes";"No";"Doesn't matter";"A"
378 DATA "Paul scolded the Corinthian church for doing what at Communion"
380 DATA "time?";"Skipping it";"Thinking only of themselves"
382 DATA "Using the wrong food";"B";"1 Cor. 11:20-22a"
384 DATA "What does Paul tell us to do before Communion?";""
386 DATA "Sing and worship";"Listen to a sermon"
388 DATA "Check ourselves for sin, and confess what we find";"C"
390 DATA "1 Corinthians 11:28,31-32"
392 DATA "In light of 1 Corinthians 11:33-34, why do we not let little kids"
394 DATA "take Communion?";"They might spill something"
396 DATA "They'd think mainly about getting to eat"
398 DATA "They're in Children's Church instead";"B";"1 Cor. 11:33-34"
```

(Note: This was written in Applesoft BASIC. Some changes may be needed for this to work on other computers, e.g., change HTAB 7 to PRINT TAB (7), HOME to CLS, etc.)

Why God Deserves the Best

The first few times a child does something in public that can be called ministry—sings a song in a church program, let's say, or visits a nursing home—he or she naturally gives top effort. It's a great honor to serve God when you're not even an adult yet. Kids give it all they've got. Later on, as the fifth and sixth and tenth opportunities come along, they find out that getting ready to minister can be work. Songs have to be practiced. Words have to be memorized. You have to make yourself stand still, on *two* feet. Grown-ups keep saying things like "Concentrate now, pay attention, just one more time."

But why? After all, this isn't school, where you get graded on your performance. The nice grandmothers in church will pat you on the head and say, "You did fine!" even if you didn't. So why bear down?

Our family had an honest talk about this one night after singing in a church the previous Sunday morning. We hadn't done poorly, but it wasn't our best, either. And Mom and Dad's recent attempts to shape up the music had sounded too much like harangues.

The line of discussion went as follows:

"On a scale of 1 to 10, how did you feel about your ministry last Sunday morning?" Each person gave a number ranking.

"Was there anything you wish could have been different?"

"Our family seems to have a tough time *getting ready* to minister. Any ideas why?"

We then read two obscure Scriptures about God's opinion of less-than-the-best offerings:

- Leviticus 22:17-22 (Family devotions out of Leviticus?! This once, yes.) "Do not bring anything with a defect. . . . Do not offer to the Lord the blind, the injured or the maimed."

This was easy enough to understand. If a friend offered to give our family a dog for a pet, but it turned out to have a broken leg or fleas, we wouldn't be terribly thrilled.

- Malachi 1:6-8, 12-14, where God roundly scolds the people for trying to get by with crippled sacrifices. "Try offering them to your governor! Would he be pleased with you? Would he accept you?"

The clinching point: When we stand in front of an audience or do any kind of ministry, we are not really trying to please the smiling grandmothers. That's not the main point. We are presenting something to the Almighty God of the Universe—and it had better be our best. Is something less worthy good enough for our Lord and Savior?

Kids in Charge for a Night

The older your children become, the more often they can plan and present a Home Together Night teaching. This heightens their interest and also develops leadership skills.

If you're a Sunday school teacher of children, you probably have access to Bible pictures, flannelgraph packets, and finger puppets. These venerable teaching aids may be old hat to adults, but kids are not as jaded. Our girls have several times presented a flannelgraph Bible story on family night, manipulating the characters and carrying on the dialogue with animation, which forces them to get the details of a Bible story straight. You may have to help them as they prepare, and you'll also need to guide them toward a summary sentence: "This story shows us that ________________."

When they finish, applaud with vigor. Then ask some follow-up questions, usually starting with the word *why.* "Why did Paul and Silas sing in the jail?" or "How come Jacob didn't tell the truth when he went in to see Isaac?" Be sure to finish with warm compliments for a job well done.

As our son has approached the teen years and suddenly discovered the world of contemporary Christian music, we have worked to prevent polarization ("your music" and "my music"). The sounds are more intense and electronic than Mom and Dad have grown up with, but isn't that to be expected? The arts keep changing, and young people are forever pushing the frontiers established by their elders (Grace and Dean remember playing "Christian folk music" twenty-five years ago that almost traumatized some members of the older generation. Now the shoe is on the other foot!)

The core of any song, we believe, is its lyrics. And we are genuinely grateful for the depth and insight of many of the contemporary

Christian lyricists. Maybe they could do with fewer amplifiers—but *what* they're saying is often good.

To highlight this, as well as to keep the bridges down in our family, we've invited Nathan to choose a song from one of his Christian tapes for presentation every other Home Together Night. He transcribes the words onto paper, makes copies for us all, and sometimes comes up with Scriptures that form a background for what Michael W. Smith or Amy Grant or Petra is saying.

Then, in our Circle Time, he plays the song, and we talk together about its meaning. We delve into the subtle phrases, the little twists of meaning, and the main idea. This gets all of us beyond the beat and instrumentation to appreciate the content. We all benefit.

Seizing the Teachable Moment

Sometimes the unexpected moment hands us the choicest opportunity. If we are spiritually awake, we may find our children more receptive because of something that's happened than they would ever be in a classroom.

A frequent example is bedtime. We parents usually have one goal in mind: get the light out! Any dawdling, stalling, or procrastinating is met with stern reminders to *hustle.*

But the child, on the other hand, is now wrapping up his or her day. The young mind often returns to something significant that happened, or something troubling—something that needs to be shared. If we will take a few seconds to be a *listener,* not just an enforcer of a certain hour on the clock, we often find ourselves in the midst of a teachable moment.

The same phenomenon sometimes pops up on Home Together Night. We have certainly missed a number of these. Here are a few we caught:

We had just gotten ice cream cones and were coming out of the store on a warm summer evening when three teenage boys came up the sidewalk. The middle one was obviously the drunkest, although his two friends were none too steady.

As they got closer, the middle boy went down—flat on his face on the concrete. The other two helped him back up, and they continued toward the corner.

"What's going on, Dad? What was wrong with that kid?"

"Well," Dean replied, "there you see the *second* half of the beer commercial. That's the part they don't show you between innings of the ball game on TV."

No planned lecture on the devastating effects of alcohol could have been as effective as the impromptu conversation that followed.

Their dismay and revulsion was almost visible on their faces as we walked toward our car.

On another summer Tuesday, Dean was overseas on a research trip, and it so happened that our church's associate pastor was also gone, lecturing at a Philippine Bible college. The two moms and six children then joined forces, piling into one car to invade the local Pizza Hut.

The roadway was undergoing construction, and the evening traffic was heavy. Belinda chose an entrance that looked passable but wasn't. Suddenly there was a thud, and her car was hung up: one set of wheels on firm asphalt, the other hanging over a two-foot ditch.

Oh, for a husband!

She became understandably distraught as she stood staring at her predicament. Meanwhile, Grace took the half-dozen kids to a grassy place nearby and said, "Let's get into a circle and pray for help." As the traffic kept whizzing by, they called out to the Lord.

Two friends from the church "happened by" the scene almost right away, and soon Belinda's car was freed with minimal damage to the undercarriage. It took longer for her nerves to calm down, so the others aided her by taking turns thanking the Lord aloud for providing assistance and for protection from injury. The children thought up encouraging praise choruses to sing in the car while riding home.

They learned more that evening about the Lord's watchfulness than whatever was waiting on the Home Together Night plan back at home. "Call upon me in the day of trouble; I will deliver you," God says in Psalm 50:15. They did, and he did.

Another evening's accident at a drop-off *did* bring injury to life and limb. That time it was a sunken piece of sidewalk that sent young Nathan, only newly able to balance a bicycle, flying into space. He landed not in the grass but on the concrete, and when he rolled over, his nose and cheek were a mass of blood.

Every parent knows what happens next: the crying, the

shrieking, the cleaning up, the medicating, the bandaging, the hugging and loving, all amid loud protests that the child will never touch a bicycle again for the rest of his life.

By the next evening, which was Tuesday, his face had swelled up terribly, but it had also become clear that there was no fracture or major damage. He looked like a child abuse victim, but in time his scabs would go away and he'd be fine.

So we turned to a new memory verse for this kind of occasion: Psalm 46:1. "God is our refuge and strength, a very present help in trouble (KJV)."

What's a "refuge"? We demonstrated the meaning of that new word by setting up three candles. The middle one, however, we planted in a gob of Play-Doh inside a tall drinking glass. The other two stood in the open air.

We lit all three wicks and then said, "Now, here comes the 'trouble.' Let's all blow hard." Two flames went out, one stayed burning because it had a "refuge." We thanked the Lord together for protecting Nathan from any permanent damage.

Ever since, that Scripture has been known in our house as "the bike accident verse."

Dean neglected a household chore one spring—checking to make sure the basement window drains were clear—and paid for it dearly. Came the July night when thunderstorms deluged our area with more than four inches of rain.

By midnight, we suddenly heard water gushing in around a window casing, cascading down onto our newly finished, carpeted rec room. We battled the flood for the next four hours, trying to stem the tide with homemade sandbags, moving furniture out of the way, sweeping the dirty water toward a floor drain, and losing ground all the time. Finally, exhausted, we retreated to bed and gave up.

By the dawn's early light the rains had stopped, and cleanup efforts resumed. In the end, we did not lose nearly as much as we had feared and were even able to save the carpeting.

The next Home Together Night, we held our Circle Time

around a chalkboard in the still-drying-out basement. "We've all been through a real mess down here," Dean said. "But let's see if we can learn anything from this. What are some lessons from our flood?"

The list included:

1. Dad should be more responsible to check the drains each year.
2. If we'd lost everything in the basement, we would still have had each other. Material things aren't as important as people.
3. In the middle of trouble, things often look worse than they turn out to be. So don't jump to conclusions and think it's the end of the world.

There have, of course, been numerous times when a Home Together Night has included prayer for the sick, either someone in our own family or else a relative or friend. (For other examples of teachable moments spawned by current happenings in the family, see "Riding the Wind" and "After a Suicide.")

Part Four
Conclusion

Seven Keys to a Successful Family Night

The preceding pages have given a shopping center of ideas for spiritual nurturing. Now it's time to retreat to the parking lot and think.

The most important point to be made is what we said in the first chapter, and we must repeat it here: *DO NOT USE THE CONTENTS OF THIS BOOK IN ISOLATION! Only as you mix them into the warm climate of family fun will they be effective.*

As you strolled the aisles of this book you may have thought, "My goodness, these people really lay it on their kids." That's a normal reaction—*if you forget* that most of these ideas were only 20 percent (or less) of an evening of food, games, excursions, jokes, and other frolic.

Parents earn the attention of their children for serious matters by showing their love for the light-hearted.

Hence:

Key No. 1 for a successful family night: Mix it up.

Keep the balance that was outlined in chapter 1, and make sure all elements pass the test of "Will a kid think this is enjoyable?"

Key No. 2: Decide what version of the Bible you're going to use, and make sure everyone has his or her own copy.

Nothing derails a reading time so much as not being able to follow along.

Our personal preferences are:

1. The New International Version (Zondervan), which is generally clear to a child and yet won't be outgrown as the teenage and adult years come. It combines the best of all worlds—although you will have to do some explaining of difficult passages at times.

2. The Good News Bible (Thomas Nelson and the American Bible Society), a translation in simple English. The line drawings throughout the book capture the action of the story, so children are led into the text.

3. The International Children's Version (Sweet), a simpler translation done to a third-grade reading level. Not as free-wheeling as a paraphrase, yet very clear.

Both the New International Version and The International Children's Version have colorful maps and helpful but not overwhelming footnotes.

There are other fine translations, of course, and you can make your family night succeed with almost any of them. Just make your choice and follow through on it.

Key No. 3: Let the children take the lead as soon and as often as they will.

Whenever they get the urge to plan or present something on Home Together Night, be it spiritual or general, say, "Great!" (Several of the ideas in this book mention this; for example, "Rx for the Christmas Carousel" and "Kids in Charge.") Kids can even teach their parents certain skills. One night, all three of our children taught us paper-folding tricks they'd picked up somewhere (probably during math class). Beautiful birds and assorted other wonders emerged. Another night at the park, they tutored Mom and Dad on the fine points of soccer (we flunked). Still they loved being in the driver's seat.

Be alert to any clues of things your children can share from their Sunday school classes, youth clubs at church, or their own personal devotions. If they're working on a project or achievement, piggyback on that; the rest of the family can help locate the Scriptures needed or brainstorm ideas together. The home and church might as well help each other instead of working separately.

Key No. 4: Keep varying the locations.

Eat in the backyard, in the dining room, on a blanket on the floor, around a Ping-Pong table or a fireplace if you're fortunate enough to have one, even in a bedroom.

Use the same variety of locations for the teaching time. Form your circle anywhere—indoors or out. If you have a wall chalkboard, gather there sometimes. Or use a portable one you keep behind the sofa.

All this adds spark and intrigue.

Key No. 5: Never stop scavenging ideas. Never lose your family night folder.

You simply cannot sit down alone, stare into space, and come up with a winner fifty-two weeks a year. You must have a collection of resources to turn to.

As we've said before, these range from fun recipes clipped from the newspaper to ideas on the backs of Sunday school papers to bright-idea notes of your own jotted at odd moments. More curriculum publishers are now providing parents suggestions to reinforce what's happening in the classroom on Sundays.

Several times Grace has found a moving Christmas story in *Guideposts* magazine that became our teaching for the night. Dean once snagged an account from *Jubilee* (the Prison Fellowship newsletter) about a woman in jail who became a Christian and decided to write a letter of confession to the widow of a federal judge she helped murder. Did they all live happily ever after? *No.* The widow turned the private letter over to her attorney, and the woman ended up getting a thirty-year sentence. But she still believes she did the God-honoring thing. Point: Confessing what we've done wrong is sometimes really tough, but living with secret guilt is even tougher.

We would never have been able to present this powerful story if the newsletter hadn't been saved in a folder.

Key No. 6: Don't let illness or fatigue stop you.

Most of the time, family night can still happen if a child or adult is sick. Granted, you may have to modify your plans, do something quieter, postpone a trip somewhere, and perhaps make the evening briefer. But the time can also take on a special quality of caring and loving as you reach out to the person in bed, pray together for healing, and find ways to show compassion.

Fatigue and the general hassles of life can also dampen your enthusiasm. You're not always going to "feel like" doing a family night. Events will come along that make it very hard to exude your usual bounce. Crises on the job, financial pressures, a too-packed schedule, and other worries can occupy adult minds.

The beauty of being a genuine family, however, is that everything does not have to be rosy for you to love each other. We remember a particularly stressful set of weeks when Grace's father was gravely ill. She and her mother were at the hospital every day, sometimes for most of the day. Many things went undone at home. Then, his condition worsened, and death seemed imminent.

Grace didn't feel at all like having Home Together Night that week—and in fact tried to get Dean to cancel it. He, however, decided to go ahead with reading some psalms together. He talked about going through hard times and then asked the children to select topics of former *good* times for slide watching (their babyhood, a Minnesota camping trip with Grandpa and Grandma, and so forth). Though Grace was physically and emotionally drained, the slides seemed to lift her spirits and pull her attention away to better days.

We can be realistic about life. We *can* confide some of our adult concerns to the whole family for prayer. We don't have to avalanche them with the weight of the world, but we do need to stay real before them and approach a loving Father for help.

It is true that single parents have a tougher time mustering the energy and time for a family night. But it can be done, and is being done. In fact, this proves to be part of the glue that mends the cracks in a home where someone has left. It says to the children, "We're still a family after all. We belong to each other. We're a group."

Key No. 7: Enhance the family night idea with symbols.

That's part of why we dreamed up a special name at our house: Home Together Night. Things that have definite names, colors, insignias, protocols, and so forth carry more definition in the participants' minds. They become things to count on.

We've also given our Home Together Night a theme song: "Feeling at Home in the Presence of Jesus," an early Gaither tune. We soon memorized the words and sang it every week for years—with guitar, with piano, with nothing, at home during Circle Time, or while working on a project, or riding in the car to something else, or at the end of the evening. More recently, we sing the song only occasionally. But it always generates warm feelings, partly because of its lyrics and partly just because it's "ours."

Other possible theme songs: "I'm So Glad I'm a Part of the Family of God," "Oh, How He Loves You and Me," "We're Together Again," "Oh, I Love You with the Love of the Lord," or another favorite of your family.

"Does It Do Any Good?"

We had no idea when we became parents fifteen years ago that the enterprise was so major. Of course we knew there was "responsibility" (a vague notion in our heads), which we assumed meant making trips to the doctor, providing food and clothing, and buying larger houses and cars than the two of us would otherwise have required.

We also knew we intended to have "a Christian home." We valued the Christian homes in which we had been raised and meant ours to be much the same.

We were so naive.

Within eight months Dean had been slapped with the realization that the work of fathering would test his own inner character to the core. Beyond making the *child* into something worthwhile, it would reveal what the *adult* was made of. A particular June day still hangs in his memory: Grace had gone shopping, the infant son would not stop crying, and the angry grown man found himself closer to losing control than he had ever dreamed possible.

A Scripture floated up from somewhere in his memory: ". . . Let every man be. . . slow to wrath: For the wrath of man worketh not the righteousness of God" (James 1:19-20, KJV). He held his son, paced the floor, and clung to restraint until Grace returned.

In the years since then, we have learned a lot. A lot about kids. A lot about ourselves. A lot about God. We have known thousands of joyous moments along with the tough times. Through it all, we have gained great respect for the parenting process. We have come to understand what psychologist W. Peter Blitchington wrote:

> No one is indispensable or irreplaceable at work. . . . Anyone, from the lowliest yardworker to the highest executive, could easily

> be replaced and few tears would be shed. The most important position in the U.S.—the presidency—is rotated every four years with little mourning. But try replacing a son or daughter, mother or father, a husband or wife without grave psychological damage. For it's in our homes that we are needed; it's to our families that we are important.[1]

Now we have written a book about our still-unfinished adventure. We have taken a risk. After all, we are not done parenting yet. We cannot point to three grown children and say, "See our marvelous results!" We cannot guarantee that all our Home Together Nights will produce the mature godliness for which we pray.

But if we waited until the votes were counted and the "proof" was in hand, we would have forgotten what these years were really like. We would be aging experts. Instead, we wanted to share our attempts and ideas now, for the benefit of others just like us.

Once, in a couples' class at a Presbyterian church, we were speaking about family night, telling much of what we've told here and urging parents to get started. At the end, an older gentleman near the back stood up. His hair was graying; his family was raised. With tears in his eyes, he said softly, "I'd just like to add one thing: Do it. *Do* it, people. My wife and I wish we could have those years over again, but we can't. And our children have not followed in the way of Christ. I can't tell you how I wish I had done these kinds of things with my children. Nothing is more important."

He said what William Barclay wrote in one book:

> The New Testament knows nothing about religious education and nothing about schools, for the New Testament is certain that the only training which really matters is given within the home, and that there are no teachers so effective for good or evil as parents are.[2]

Is he overstretching the point? Not if we take note of the statistic that a young person up through age eighteen spends only 7.6 percent of his or her life in school (12,000 hours). Television watching, on the other hand—a home activity—claims 9 percent (15,000 hours).

In other words, it's up to us. Not only scholastically, but morally, spiritually, and in most other ways as well. For these twenty years or so, raising mature Christian kids must be our first occupation. Yes, we have to earn money to do that, but the priority must be clear. If we ignore our God-given assignment, there's no backup system. And the calendar keeps turning.

So will the ingredients of this book do any good? We cannot give money-back guarantees. Parenting is too complex for that sort of thing. It is simply our wish to stand before God someday and be able to say, "We gave it our best shot. We did what we knew to do." From there on, the results are beyond us.

But the children are in good hands. We can be "confident of this, that he who began a good work in you will carry it on to completion until the day of Christ Jesus" (Phil. 1:6). He and we are partners together, and we are building nothing less than specimens of godly excellence. He is more than our final Judge. He is our Senior Advisor right now. He is on our side. We are in this together.

Together at home.

---

[1] W. Peter Blitchington, *Sex Roles and the Christian Family* (Wheaton, Ill.: Tyndale, 1980), 48.

[2] William Barclay, *Train Up a Child: Educational Ideals in the Ancient World* (Philadelphia: Westminster, 1959), 236.